Henry Jacobs

A Lay of the Southern Cross and other Poems

Henry Jacobs

A Lay of the Southern Cross and other Poems

ISBN/EAN: 9783337253424

Printed in Europe, USA, Canada, Australia, Japan

Cover: Foto ©Thomas Meinert / pixelio.de

More available books at **www.hansebooks.com**

A Lay of the Southern Cross,

AND OTHER POEMS.

A Lay of the Southern Cross

AND OTHER POEMS.

BY

THE VERY REV. HENRY JACOBS, D.D.,

DEAN OF CHRIST CHURCH, NEW ZEALAND,

FORMERLY MICHEL FELLOW OF QUEEN'S COLLEGE, OXFORD,

AUTHOR OF "COLONIAL CHURCH HISTORIES—NEW ZEALAND, S.P.C.K."

SKEFFINGTON & SON, PICCADILLY, LONDON,

Publishers to H.R.H. the Prince of Wales,

AND

A. WHITE, BOOKSELLER, VICTORIA ST., CHRISTCHURCH, NEW ZEALAND.

—

1893.

TO THOSE PATRIOTIC SPIRITS,

WHOSE HEARTS GOD HAS STIRRED

TO AIM AT THE REGENERATION OF THEIR RACE,

THE WRITER OF THIS POEM

DEDICATES THIS HUMBLE EFFORT

WITH GENUINE ADMIRATION,

WITH HEARTFELT SYMPATHY,

AND WITH THE EARNEST PRAYER,

THAT GOD MAY BLESS THEIR ENDEAVOURS,

TO RAISE UP THEIR COUNTRYMEN

TO OCCUPY AN HONOURED PLACE

IN THE CHRISTENDOM OF THE TWENTIETH CENTURY.

PREFACE.

SHOULD you be curious to know, dear Reader, why this Poem was written, it is no conceit, but the honest truth to say, that I was impelled to write it. I might almost say, "I could not help it." I undertook in February, 1886, by desire of those whose request was an honour and a command, the task of writing the History of the Church of New Zealand,* and in my preparation for the work became simply enamoured of the wondrous tale of the evangelization of the country, which may be described as a Religious Romance. The more I read, the more my admiration grew, until at length it broke out in song. I communicated my secret to very few; for I was afraid lest my enthusiasm should fail, or grow cold. But it was not so; on the contrary, the work became more and more a comfort to me, and a support under severe mental trials and bodily illness. It has never been a hindrance to my duties; for it became my chief refreshment. I very seldom sat down to elaborate any portion of it; for I composed almost the whole of it in the course of my walks, or when I was dressing, or on wet days, as I walked up and down for exercise : and the results were committed to paper as opportunity offered. But why publish it, you may ask? Well, I humbly hope that this, and the other shorter poems, which help to make up this volume, and which have been written under similar circumstances, on various occasions in the course of nearly half a lifetime, may be accepted, through the dear Lord Jesus Christ, as a thank-offering to our Heavenly Father, and be made use of by Him, as He knows best, for the good of His Church.

* "*Colonial Church Histories: New Zealand.*" *By the Very Rev. Henry Jacobs, D.D., Dean of Christchurch, N.Z. (S.P.C.K.)*

CONTENTS.

A LAY OF THE SOUTHERN CROSS.

Canto I.

MARSDEN.

I.

"WHO were those men, my Father?   From what race
   Sprang they?   So noble looking, but so wild?
Yet, as I looked, methought mine eye could trace
   In those swarth features something of a mild
Melancholy."   "New Zealand chiefs, my child;
   They are indeed a noble race, but oh!
So steeped in ignorance, and so defiled
   By brutish superstitions, sunk so low—
What power on earth can lift them from such depth of woe?"

A

II.

"There is a power, my Father." "Yes, my child—
    The grace of Him that died upon the Cross—
That, that alone can cleanse the sin-defiled ;
    And now, my daughter, list ! As I did toss
Last night upon my bed, the seeming loss
    Of night's brief rest to me was gain untold,
Which straightway turned all earthly gains to dross ;
    Before my mind such visions did unfold
Of a whole nation born, and in God's Book enrolled.

III.

"I saw the portal of the Kingdom ope
    And dark throngs pressing in, their foreheads signed
With gleaming crosses, and—I humbly hope
    I am not wrong in telling—to my mind,
Not to mine ear, there breathed a whispering wind,
    'Apostle of New Zealand thou shalt be :'
I am content to do His will, resigned
    To spend, be spent, whate'er the cost may be,
To seek for Him those Islanders beyond the sea."

IV.

Thus Samuel Marsden to his daughter speaks,
    The convicts' Chaplain he of New South Wales ;
Who ne'er his own, but others' welfare seeks ;
    From hardship shrinks not, nor at danger quails :
Whose stubborn perseverance never fails ;
    Wise as the serpent, harmless as the dove ;
Champion of right, though ill-repute assails,
    Or good emboldens ; scorn he meets with love ;
Nor threats, nor foul abuse, his resolution move.*

* See "Memoirs of the Life and Labours of the Rev. Samuel Marsden," edited by the Rev. J. B. Marsden, M.A., (R.T.S.); and "Colonial Church Histories—New Zealand," by the Very Rev. H. Jacobs, D.D. (S.P.C.K.), Ch. i., pp. 3, 4.

V.

At Paramatta is his Parsonage,
   And there he builds a simple hostelry,
To lodge New Zealanders of every age,
   Who, led by eager curiosity,
The works and ways of Sydney come to 'spy;
   And thus he wins their hearts; each guest imbibes
Warm gratitude for hospitality;
   And, home returning, to his name ascribes
Renown, which spreads as sweetest perfume through the
     tribes.

VI.

But ah! this kindness brings anxiety;
   One day the Chaplain was from home; there died
A chieftain's nephew; soul-society
   The soul departing needs—so Satan lied—
"My servant must be slain," the chieftain cried,
   "To bear him company." Miss Marsden ran
Quicker than thought: "Haste! Henga, haste thee, hide
   In yonder room; I'll shield thee all I can,
Until my father come, and stay that dreadful man."

VII.

The chief relented at the Chaplain's word:
   Yet hardly, grieved at loss of dignity
As well as comfort, by the youth incurred;
   "How should he meet his sire's reproachful eye?"
That night unto his God did Marsden cry,
   "O Lord, how long ere Thy salvation's power
Shall shew its lighting down, and bring them nigh
   That under darkness and death's shadow cower?
Lord, send Thy Holy Ghost, and haste redemption's hour."

VIII.

Nor prayed he only, but watched Providence,
    When it should grant blest opportunity ;
And, by-and-bye, affairs of consequence
    Took him to London, where in unity
Seeking to save each lost community,
    A zealous body sent on every hand
Its missions to reclaim humanity—
    To Greenland's shores, or " India's coral strand,"
Or where dark " Afric's fountains pour their golden sand."

IX.

He thus addressed them : " Hear me, Reverend Sirs,
    And Christian brethren, hear my strong appeal ;
I am no speaker, but a spirit stirs
    Within me, ardent, restless, and I feel
I must the burden of my soul reveal.
    There lies a land beneath the Southern Cross,
Whose thousand sins and sorrows none can heal
    But He Who 'suffered to redeem our loss ; '
His Word alone can bring them out of darkness gross.

X.

" Its name, New Zealand ; and on that fair land
    Blest with mild climate and a fertile soil,
Great God hath poured His gifts with lavish hand,
    Nor aught withholds of good ; needs but the toil
Of man to make it teem with olive oil,
    Honey and milk, rich fruits and waving grain ;
Prowls there no savage beast, nor hideous coil
    Of snake unwinds ; but ah ! more hideous train
Of Eden's primal serpent wreathes and coils amain.

XI.

"There tribal jealousy, ancestral feud,
  Each year begetting fresh revenge and hate,
Are rife ; the vehemence of passion lewd
  Murder begets, lewd passion's sworn co-mate ;
Such fury once excited nought can sate,
  But—horrible to say !—the savage taste
Of human flesh and blood ; so desolate
  By Satan's hand this Eden, and defaced,
As sometime by fierce boar fair vineyards are laid waste.

XII.

"Yet is their temper naturally kind,
  Their features with a genial radiance lit ;
A finer, nobler race you scarce will find ;
  Of strong and agile frame, limbs firmly knit ;
And of a marvellously sprightly wit ;
  Bright, lovable, emotional, yet mild :
To take the impress of high culture fit ;
  Faithful to friend, tender to wife and child ;
Like flow'rs which erstwhile bloomed in gardens, now run
      wild.

XIII.

"Up, brethren, banded in the Mission cause :
  Up, recognize your hour ; our Master calls :
Conquer for Him that land, and to His laws
  Subdue that people : those poor captive thralls
Of Satan rescue ; then within the walls
  Of our blest home, Jerusalem above,
Shall sound melodious strains ; e'en now there falls
  Upon mine ears their echo ; ye who prove
His goodness daily, up, and teach them 'God is love.'"

XIV.

He ceased; and, sitting down, a modest flush
　O'erspread his manly features, as the sun,
Sinking, illumes the west with vivid blush:
　Now mark the murmuring approbation run
Around that seated board, as when on one
　Of autumn's sultriest days the insect-whirr
Makes the air vocal.　Their assent is won:
　Yet are there many doubts: they fear to err
Through rashness; for the rein is needful as the spur—

XV.

The rein of caution, as the spur of zeal.
　Up rose the Chairman presently, and spake:
"We thank you, Reverend Sir, for your appeal;
　We feel its force; your stirring words awake
Our heartiest sympathy; and for His sake,
　Who came from Heaven to seek and save the lost,
The solemn charge we gladly undertake;
　But, ere we make the plunge, this thought has crossed
Our minds, 'Ere ye begin this work, count well the cost.'

XVI.

" How to attack the work?　How best begin?
　Needs there no common forethought and design.
A general that would a city win,
　Makes slow approach by stratagem and mine:
So must sound judgment with our zeal combine.
　Therefore, dear brother, thy advice we crave.
The foe is strong and wily; but divine
　Courage and strength are pledged, if we are brave;
Work on, trust God, and pray; and He is strong to save."

XVII.

Again the murmuring admiration ran
    Around that board. With spirit greatly cheered
And heart emboldened, rose that reverend man ;
    And thus he spake, "O brethren much endeared
In bonds of Christian fellowship, I feared
    Not lack of fervent zeal, but chilling doubt
Of overcoming obstacles that reared
    Their giant forms, and power to carry out
Designs that need resources vast within, without.

XVIII.

"That question I have pondered o'er and o'er—
    How to attack the work ? how best begin ?
And pondering has convinced me more and more,
    That, ere religion can a footing win,
The arts must lead the way, and, entering in,
    Must tame and civilize, cause wars to cease,
Supply new motives, and so wean from sin,
    Charm by the richness of the earth's increase,
Turn spears to pruning hooks, and clubs to tools of peace.*

XIX.

" Wherefore to this my counsel, Sirs, give heed :
    Look out three artisans of good report,
Men skilled in works of ordinary need,
    And yet not men of ordinary sort ;
Men who in trouble to their God resort,
    Yet men of action, resolute and brave,
And, if it may be, men of goodly port.
    These, teaching useful arts, the way shall pave,
For holy truths and discipline, men's souls to save.

* See " Colonial Church Histories—New Zealand," p. 6.

XX.

"Choose me such men, and I will place them where
    The tribes are densest, 'neath a sunny sky,
Northeastward, in the Bay of Islands fair,
    Where sheltered whalers stormy blasts defy ;
Where Sydney merchantmen their traffic ply ;
    There must they live hard lives, and day by day,
Like Baptists in the wilderness, must cry,
    'We come to usher in a better day ;
A Kingdom cometh soon ; we but prepare the way.'"

XXI.

Again he ceased ; brief silence then ensued,
    As though of doubt ; then rose throughout the hall
Discordant murmurs, as of men who viewed
    This counsel variously : thus ofttimes fall
The gusts at midnight ; then a sudden squall
    Rustles the tree-tops. So that keen debate
Stirred every zealous heart, till well-nigh all
    Assented ; but the doubtful said, " We wait
To watch the issue, and repair, ere yet too late."

XXII.

One William Hall they found ; the trade he plied
    Erstwhile ennobled by th' incarnate Lord
In Nazareth's blest shade, and his beside,
    The patriarch-shipbuilders, who took on board
The world's sole hope. For ever be adored
    His Holy Name, Who raised up simple folk
That for the love of souls self-love abhorred,
    Took on them once for all the Master's yoke,
Nor did, till life was o'er, the choice once made revoke.

XXIII.

With him a shoemaker, John King by name,
    With preparation of the Gospel shod,
The Gospel of meek peace, invited came
    To share the holy warfare for his God :
Taught had he been in youth to bear the rod :
    Knew he to strip the flax, and twist the yarn
For ropes and fishing nets : to till the sod,
    And plough and sow, and gather into barn ;
Yet apt to teach, reprove, admonish, comfort, warn.

XXIV.

Time passed ; and now the needments were prepared
    For the far voyage ; long farewells were said
By loving friends.   Some no endeavours spared
    To stay them, and had made their hearts afraid,
But that their trust was on th' Almighty stayed :
    Some said, "God speed; the Lord be with you both ;
Since you, we know, the cost have duly weighed ;
    Although to lose your presence we are loth,
What skills that loss to God's own glorious Kingdom's
      growth ?"

XXV.

Once more the missionary senior's met,
    Of Marsden to take courtly Christian leave,
And to exhort those catechists.   When set,
    The Chairman rose and said, " Dear Sir, we grieve
To say farewell : we would that some reprieve,
    Though brief, were granted ; but right well we know
Your work demands your presence ; Sir, believe
    We all shall pray that, wheresoe'er you go,
The Lord will shield you well, and bless whate'er you do.

XXVI.

"This, your own mission, we commend to you;
　　Regard it as the apple of your eye;
For needful means in vain you shall not sue:
　　Watch o'er these men; in hour of need supply
Comfort and aid from nearer Australie;
　　And, as time passes, if it be God's will,
Go, cheer and bless them with society;
　　Fresh courage in their drooping hearts instil,
As at fond parents' sight fond children's bosoms thrill."

XXVII.

Then to those workmen-catechists he turned,
　　And said, "Dear brothers, ye may rightly guess
The fulness of our hearts, how they have burned
　　For you, now sent into the wilderness;
Heed, Sirs, the lessons we would now impress:
　　First, be ye men of God; His kingdom seek,
As paramount; seek growth in holiness;
　　Be strong in faith, but in self-trust be weak;
By yielding conquer; victory is for the meek.

XXVIII.

"To piety add patient industry:
　　Religion's handmaid, Art, will smooth the way
For her more welcome entrance; as you ply
　　Your several trades, bethink you oft to say
A word in season, that th' onlookers may
　　While bent on sport, drink wisdom unawares;
You, Hall, to wit, whene'er you fell a tree,
　　Say, when you know their language, 'Thus it fares
With man once fall'n; thenceforth nor fruit nor leaves he
　　　　bears:

XXIX.

"'Make then the most of life.' And you, John King,
  May deftly make Christ's Parables your own,
Pointing the moral of each simple thing—
  How faulty soil oft mars the good seed sown ;
How plants grow wild and useless, left alone—
  Cultured, increase for profit and delight ;
Or how with noxious weeds the bed o'ergrown,
  That was with fragrant loveliness bedight,
Resembles man's condition in his Maker's sight ;

XXX.

"When the child-soul, from active sin once pure,
  Is fouled by crimes and superstitions vile.
But chiefly, brothers, strive ye to allure
  The children of that bright but crime-stained Isle
By pure example : let no spot defile
  The likeness which we all profess to bear
Of Him that saved us—Now, Sirs, kneel, the while
  We humbly crave in strong, united prayer
For them and for their work God's kind protective care."

XXXI.

They knelt ; and in impressive words he prayed
  That God would bless the arduous enterprise ;
That those brave men might never be afraid
  What man could do to them ; be bold, yet wise ;
That He, in danger's hour, would heed their cries ;
  That, dying, they might reap a rich reward.
He ceased ; then Marsden prayed ; then all arise,
  And all, with hearts uplifted to the Lord,
Sing these, or such like fervent words, with one accord.

THE HYMN OF THE MISSION COMMITTEE.

I.

Rise up, O God, at length
  Bring on the expected hour;
Let Thy right arm light down in strength,
  And shatter Satan's power.
    Haste, oh! haste the hoped-for whitening
      Of Thy harvest, Lord, we pray;
    Speed, oh! speed the longed-for brightening—
      Dawn of the Eternal Day.

II.

Oh! wherefore hast Thou framed
  So many souls for nought;
For Jesus be those souls reclaimed
  Which by His blood were bought!
    Haste, oh! haste the wished-for whitening
      Of Thy harvest, Lord, we pray:
    Speed, oh! speed the longed-for brightening—
      Dawn of the Eternal Day.

III.

Thou hast ordained that man
  To man the light should bring:
Free hand we on, as free began
  That light from Thee to spring!
    Haste, oh! haste the wished-for whitening
      Of Thy harvest, Lord, we pray:
    Speed, oh! speed the longed-for brightening—
      Dawn of the Eternal Day.

IV.

Oh ! call the outcasts in
  To bow before Thy face,
Dear fellow-citizens within
  The covenant of grace.
    Haste, oh ! haste the wished-for whitening
      Of Thy harvest, Lord, we pray :
    Speed, oh ! speed the longed-for brightening—
      Dawn of the Eternal Day.

V.

For Thee, for Thee, O Lord,
  The waiting Isles do yearn.
Make by Thy Spirit's quickening word
  Their hearts within them burn !
    Haste, oh ! haste the hoped-for whitening
      Of Thy harvest, Lord, we pray :
    Speed, oh ! speed the longed-for brightening—
      Dawn of the Eternal Day.

Canto II.

RUATARA.

I.

On board a female convict-ship, the "Ann,"
 The three embarked, ere many days were o'er;
With favouring breeze and tide they quickly ran
 Down the rich-freighted Thames unto the Nore:
And, as the river on its breast them bore,
 Marsden with talk whiled tedious hours away,
Delighting his two comrades with a store
 Of various anecdote both grave and gay,
Attaching to each spot along the historic way.

II.

First Greenwich comes in view, famed palace-home
 Of veteran seamen; Woolwich 'cross the stream,
Grand arsenal; next Gravesend, whither come
 At Easter pleasure-seeking crowds to dream
The livelong day away in joy supreme;
 Nor blames he timely mirth, relief from toil.
"How both these banks," he cries, "with memories
 teem!
 Who shall blame us, who leave our native soil,
If from her glorious records we bear off some spoil?"

III.

As Tilbury's old Fort appeared, he said,
    " Here once our good Queen Bess in martial pride,
When Spain's Armada threatened, and blood-red
    The beacons blazed, before her troops did ride."
But where broad Thames receives full Medway's tide,
    Remembering the Dutch and our disgrace,
Sudden he checked his patriot zeal, and sighed :—
    " How often in the history of a race
Disaster closely dogging sin's foul steps we trace !"

IV.

Lo ! ere the royal Thames is left behind,
    Another sad remembrance, where the Nore
Faces the Channel !   But enough ! the wind
    Bore them full swiftly down the Kentish shore,
Right through the Downs ; the lurking perils o'er
    Of Goodman's fatal Sands ; past Beachy Head ;
Thence for the Isle of Wight they eastward bore—
    Sweet sunny Isle, where he who sings was bred,
And where both parents lie, the grassy turf o'erhead. *

V.

The Needles past, and Portland's jutting Bill,
    Along the lonely Devon coast they glide :
Their wistful eyes with tears unwilling fill,
    As I have known sometime a youthful bride,
Joy of her husband's heart, her parents' pride,
    Weep, not for sorrow, but for fond regret,
As she steps forth, the bridegroom by her side,
    From her old home ; what, though her eyelids wet,
On her new life her choice and heart are fully set.

* In the Churchyard of Chale, Isle of Wight.

VI.

No ! England ! dearest mother ! not unmov'd
   Thy children e'er can leave thee : what they feel
The starting tear hath oft unbidden prov'd,
   As sudden sighs to lovers do reveal
What erst they know not.   Quenchless is their zeal
   For thy renown, and passionate and strong ;
And pray for thee they will, and seek thy weal,
   However far they roam ; however long
Their absence from thee, still their hearts thy memories
     throng.

VII.

Our voyagers, thus musing, passed the Start :
   Then Eddystone, just lighted, came in sight :
"Ah ! there is that might cheer our fainting heart ;
   See there a pledge that in your darkest night
Your God will make your darkness to be light—
   The semblance of the Church upon the Rock,
Amidst the darkness ever shining bright,
   Standing for aye unmoved 'midst error's shock,
'Gainst which the pow'rs of hell arrayed in vain shall mock."

VIII.

Marsden thus spake : " But who is this ? " he cried,
   As climbing to the forecastle to see
The Rock more clearly, outstretched there he spied
   A wretched sight, as wretched well could be,
Sunk to a state of sad debility :
   Trickled the life-blood slowly from his throat
As the hoarse coughing racked him ; languidly
   He moved his limbs, wrapped in an old great-coat,
And clouted rags, the veriest miser would devote

IX.

To ditch or flames.   Dark-skinned is he ; his face
   Embroidered with strange figures and curved lines,
Which seam his heavy lips, and interlace
   Upon his swarthy cheeks ; death's dark confines
He nears.   A woeful object ! yet are signs
   Not wanting of a strange nobility :
An air of native dignity combines
   With deep depression, as some majesty
Lingers around a king 'neath worst indignity.

X.

With manly sympathy their hearts are wrung—
   When "Marsden ! Minister !" he sudden cries :
The smooth soft accents of the Maori tongue
   Salute his ears with sorrowful surprise ;
And tears he cannot check bedew his eyes,
   As in that dark-skinned mariner, so worn,
So woe-begone, that there before him lies,
   He recognizes one to honour born,
A Maori chief, whose looks his rank did once adorn.

XI.

At Paramatta once he was a guest—
   The bright young chief of Rangihoua he—
Young Ruatara, noted for his quest
   Of knowledge, and his strong desire to see
Our England, and learn how she came to be
   So great and wise ; and how she came to grow
In strength and riches and prosperity ;
   For he would have his own New Zealand so,
With such fond love of country did his bosom glow.*

* *The name of this remarkable young man is spelt in the C.M.S. Reports, and in old books on New Zealand, thus, Duaterra.   The meaning of the word is Lizard.*

B

XII.

But ah ! this woeful change !   Ask ye the cause
    Of this adversity and misery ?
'Twas no depravity, nor broken laws
    Of God or man ; no sad calamity ;
But, sadder far ! 'twas human perfidy :
    List ye the tale of tyranny and wrong
And say if e'er such barbarous cruelty
    In all the world, through all the ages long,
Stands registered in prose, or moralized in song.

XIII.

Smitten with youthful love of novelty,
    And keen desire to visit foreign lands,
Leaving his native Bay of Islands, he
    The master of a whaling-ship's commands
Obeyed for many months ; then on the sands
    Of Sydney's harbour was he put on shore,
Of wages cheated, thrown on his own hands ;
    He must have starved, or begged from door to door,
But one in mercy took him to his home once more—

XIV.

A generous skipper he ; and now you'd think
    Young Ruatara's vagrant passion cured—
That he, once brought to destitution's brink,
    And having such vile treachery endured,
Would not again be easily allured
    To trust his freedom to another's will ;
But sooner might a torrent be immured
    By rock or bank, than hearts which visions fill
Of golden lands and wild adventures, e'er be still.

XV.

Wouldst know the bait that tempted him ?   The pledge
   "To shew him England and King George !"   This
     thought
Whetted to keenest appetite the edge
   Of youthful enterprise ; it wrought and wrought
Like yeast within his simple soul, till nought
   The ferment could allay ; yet could he wait :
What though experience dearly he had bought,
   Let but that hope be granted, then might fate
Or, worse, man's cruelty its vengeful fury sate.

XVI.

"Fill we our ship with sealskins first," he said—
   The "Santa Anna's" captain—"and with oil
Of whale, and then our gallant sails we'll spread
   For merry England, on whose glorious soil
You shall enjoy long respite without toil ;
   And you shall see King George, all clothed in gold ;
And you shall have full share of ocean's spoil
   To get fine clothes, and flaunt it gay and bold,
And see all London's mighty wonders, famed of old."

XVII.

Down to the Bounty Islands first they steer,
   A well-known playground of the phocine race,
Where sportive sea-calves gambol without fear—
   Strange clumsy creatures with half-human face,
And large soft eyes, in which you seem to trace
   Feeling and gentleness, rough though each name—
Sea-bear, sea-lion—look ! each sunny place
   Is all alive with frolic and with game
Of walrus and sea-elephant's unwieldy frame.

XVIII.

" Now here is paying work for four or five ;
 Come, then, my mates, you five on shore shall stay,"
The captain said, " and if you look alive,
 Those briny monsters you by scores shall slay ;
To Norfolk Island we will now away
 To bring provisions and fresh water back ;
Ten days once gone, expect us day by day ;
 With what I leave you, you will have no lack."
So said, he sailed away upon his northward track.

XIX.

Young Ruatara was of those thus left :
 And days and weeks elapsed, and no return—
And now they 'gan to feel themselves bereft—
 O ye deserted, whither will ye turn ?
Patience and long endurance ye must learn—
 Fierce gnawing hunger, agonies of thirst—
Hope long deferred, sickness of hearts that yearn
 For home and children, and, that torment worst,
Vain visions of relief, bubbles but formed to burst.

XX.

For ten long months he came not.   Ye who hear,
 Can ye conceive what hardships they endured ?
A rock-bound isle, so shelterless and drear
 Would make dire havoc of those most inured
To cold and heat's extremes.   Coarse sea-fowl, lured
 To their destruction, formed their scanty meat :
No water, save from heav'n, could be procured :
 Each in his turn watched from high rocky seat
For glimpse of passing sail, but each to hope's defeat.

XXI.

A few are seen, but most, alas ! too far ;
  And some draw near, then fade away from sight ;
Some steer towards them, as they watching are :
  Then signal they for help with all their might :
"Ah yes ! they see, they come, all will be right ; "
  But cruel disappointment doth make sport
Of radiant hope, and drown in dismal night
  Their thoughts of succour near.   Yet I exhort,
"Hope against hope ; " ere long will come some brief
    support.

XXII.

One came and left scant aid, but not, alas !
  Till chilling night-blasts and fell hunger's stress
Had caused three pining, suffering souls to pass
  Forth from that savage, rock-bound wilderness
To where no human hardship can oppress.
  But Ruatara's spirit, fed with hope,
Quailed with no fear, succumbed to no distress ;
  When face to face with Death, refused to mope,
And with his ghastly form dared manfully to cope.

XXIII.

So mayst thou see upon some eastward crest,
  While darkness mantles o'er full many a peak,
Upon one brow the parting sunlight rest.
  Say not his dream was trivial, nor speak
Harshly, as though his heart were vain and weak :
  Bethink thee this—canst thou, O Christian, say
Thou dost a higher realm or Monarch seek ?
  That that exalted Vision is thy stay—
The King in glory and the Land so far away ?

XXIV.

At length the captain came, and piles on piles
    Of seal-skins gladdened his gain-cankered eyes ;
Seal-skins which, stretched at length, would cover miles;
    Seal-skins of every hue and every size :
Straightway to London sailed he with his prize—
    London, the mart of nations—mighty change
From Islands, miscalled " Bounty !"   What surprise
    For Ruatara !   He at large would range,
And feast his eager eyes on all things new and strange.

XXV.

Now would he see King George enthroned in state,
    And England's glittering chieftains thronging round :
But yet awhile must long-tried patience wait
    Till full completion of his toil be crowned
By the rich freight's discharge ; set foot on ground
    He may not, till this final work be done.
Thus was his eager expectation wound
    To highest pitch ; days counted one by one
Aye nearer bring the goal of hope's fulfilment won.

XXVI.

But who can gauge the depths of selfish greed ?
    Nor adamant nor granite can compare
In hardness with the hateful, grov'lling breed
    Of world-seared hearts, that know no other care
But to be rich.   Such cruelty is rare
    E'en in the cruel, as that skipper bore
Within his fiendish soul, who did not spare
    Soon as the last and utmost task was o'er,
To turn that wretched wight adrift upon the shore—

XXVII.

Upon the pitiless quay, without a friend,
　　In London's vast and dreary solitude :
In vain did hapless Ruatara spend
　　His loud reproaches ; long but vainly sued
Fulfilment of those promises, but rude
　　Coarse laughter, savage oaths, and cruel scorn —
Hear, righteous Lord, from Heaven and judge !—
　　　　pursued
　　That helpless outcast, cut to th' heart, forlorn —
Like wrung-out orange, in the gutter flung, and torn.

XXVIII.

But brightest shines in trouble's darkest night
　　God's mercy, and, by unseen angel led,
He shipped on board the "Ann," in sorry plight,
　　To work his way for daily dole of bread,
To Sydney's wharf : here, as erstwhile 'twas said,
　　The Chaplain and his catechists discerned
His prostrate form, neglected and half-dead—
　　The barbarous crew had beaten him, they learned—
And, as they heard his tale, their hearts within them burned.

XXIX.

Now mark the power of Christian sympathy,
　　And how the lesson of th' Ascended Lord,
In loving souls is writ indelibly,
　　" Go and do likewise ; " for with one accord
Those three disciples oil of pity poured
　　On that torn spirit, soothed his aching woes
With balm of comfort, life and hope restored
　　To that worn trav'ller, fall'n 'mong cruel foes,
Half-dead, and freshly smarting from their wanton blows.

XXX.

Revived he then full soon, as I have known
　　A plant which, half-uprooted, trailing lay
In dust, lift up its head, and thankful own
　　The power of human tenderness.　Ah ! stay
To marvel at the influence mortals may
　　Exert upon each other's destiny,
For good or ill, for weal or woe ; to slay
　　Or heal ; to soothe or vex : may
Be helpers of each other's joy, not misery !

XXXI.

And now they were a goodly company,
　　And much and happily conversed, as oft
As duty done gave opportunity ;
　　When Ruatara was not up aloft,
In keeping watch, in Maori accents soft
　　Told he the marvels of his native land ;
Though feeble still, though hoarsely still he coughed,
　　Still spat forth blood, while they on either hand
Strove hard the while his broken speech to understand.

XXXII.

And ne'er in mountain-heart of Scot or Swiss
　　Did patriotic ardour livelier burn—
In spirit Greek or Roman, than in his :
　　His people's degradation deep concern
Had wakened in him ; he had striven to learn
　　All useful arts, which might avail to raise
Their abject minds from low desires, and turn
　　Their spell-bound sounds from superstition's ways,
Revenge and horrid feasts, and love of cruel frays.

XXXIII.

Not yet a child of God, and yet not far
    From the Redeemer's Kingdom ; twilight gleams
Of knowledge cheer him onward, as the Star
    Which led the Magi by its gentle beams
To where the glory, seen by angels, streams
    From out the manger-cradle of the King :
For like Epiphany in sanguine dreams
    Young Ruatara yearns ; would Christ but bring
The people of the further East beneath His wing !

XXXIV.

Nor did they miss the advantage of the time—
    Marsden and his co-mates—but plied him well
With skilful questioning, yet this object prime
    They make, to learn his speech ; then bid him tell
What Maories eat, how cook, how clothe, how dwell ;
    How they employ themselves, and what believe :
The while their hearts with thankful wonder swell,
    That God should so their pathways interweave,
That each from each should this unlooked-for good receive.

XXXV.

On their long voyage are they now well sped ;
    Through tropic calms and variable winds
By north-east Trades far southward have they fled :
    The shining Bear of home no more reminds,
But the sweet influence of the Pleiads binds
    South still to north ; Orion's flaming belt
Clasps with uniting band responsive minds ;
    And thou, dear Southern Cross, all hearts dost melt,
When first beheld, for many a loss full solace felt.

XXXVI.

One day, when they had passed the famous Cape
　　Named of Good Hope—the sun had set full aft,
And lay reposing 'neath a purple drape
　　Pillowed on crimson clouds ; fresh breezes waft
O'er amber-tinted waves the gallant craft ;
　　Sportive and free the jovial porpoise rolled,
And leapt and plunged ; and mighty Ocean laughed
　　With myriad curls and dimples manifold
O'er his broad face, amused his children to behold.

XXXVII.

Then rose the moon in splendour, and at first
　　Star to far-distant star glad welcome cried ;
Then sudden seemed the wide-spread sky to burst
　　Into effulgence, like a royal bride
Adorned with brilliants, sparkling in her pride—
　　'Twas on this glorious night the Chaplain said
To Ruatara, seated by his side,
　　With King and Hall, " My friends, to God o'erhead,
Be praise for this magnificence around us spread !

XXXVIII.

" You, King and Hall, have known the light of truth
　　Which shines from old in Anglia's happy home ;
You both have been instructed from your youth,
　　That all things come from one Almighty Hand ;
That He doth bind all nature with a band
　　Of all-preserving love : but thou, my son,
Defer not longer our oft-pressed demand ;
　　Recount, I pray, before this day is done,
The Maori Legend of Earth, Heaven, and Sky, and Sun ;

XXXIX.

"And whence the Maori sprang, how southward came:—
  But first sing we our Hymn, as we are wont:"
Then sang they this:—

A HYMN OF THE SOUTHERN OCEAN.

I.

The vast expanse of ocean, Lord,
  Proclaims how vast Thy Majesty:
Enlarge our hearts to like expanse
  With wonder, awe, and worship high.

II.

How loftily the sky above
  Uplifts her arching canopy!
O make our grov'lling spirits soar
  To more and more sublimity!

III.

Each sunrise, and each sunset too,
  Illumes the wave with flush of praise:
So may our works, in Thee begun,
  In Thee completed, gild our days!

IV.

Thy glorious constellations, Lord,
  Give all their brightness back to Thee:
So shine our light before mankind,
  That they in us Thy praise may see!

V.

How legibly upon the dark
  Thy Cross its golden nails doth print !
So may our faith and hope shine best,
  When life shows skies of blackest tint !

VI.

Leap up, glad creatures of the deep ;
  Your joys your Maker's goodness speak :
May like spontaneous joys be ours,
  When His life-giving Face we seek !

VII.

All creatures own Thee great and good,
  In depth beneath, in height above :
A closer tie Thy children feel ;
  They bless Thee for a Father's love.

VIII.

To Him Who formed the winding coast,
  The sun, the sky, the stars, the sea ;
To Father, Son, and Holy Ghost,
  All thanks and praise and glory be.
                              Amen.

Canto III.

LEGENDARY.*

I.

THEN Ruatara modestly began :
  " I know not if the words I speak are right ;
But thus our father's taught : ere yet was man,
  Ages and ages back, nought was but night ;
Night, night, black night ; no single gleam of light
  The pitchy darkness broke ; above, below,
Rangi and Papa, Heaven and Earth, were quite
  Confused, and ever did together grow,
Yet ever wrestling, restless, surging to and fro.

II.

" There wallowed in this mass six giants vast,
  Rangi and Papa's sons ; sore had they striven
For light and liberty, long ages past ;
  With ceaseless anguish were their spirits riven,
Crying, ' O give us light ; were light but given,
  We could contented die ;' yet wondered they,
What light could be.· At last, by passion driven,
  Bethought they, ' Shall we now our parents slay,
Or rend asunder, to let in the light of day ?'

* My principal authority for the singular legends related in this Canto is
" Polynesian Mythology," by Sir George Grey.

III.

" Then cried Tumatauenga, fiercest he
 Of all the giant brood, ' Up, let us slay ;'
But Tane, father of the forest tree,
 And all that grows within the wood, cried, ' Nay,
Let us not kill, but rend apart, I say :
 Let us send Rangi up, force Papa down ;
Then shall we gain the wished-for light of day ;
 Then shall we win of all our hopes the crown,
To stock this mighty void with offspring of our own.'

IV.

" Four brothers roared assent ; the fifth opposed—
 Lord of the whistling wind and howling blast—
For much he feared, lest he should be deposed
 From his dominion, were the severance past :
Stormed he with all his tempests, but at last
 It was determined ; yet four strove in vain
To achieve the rending ; through the abysmal vast
 Rangi and Papa's laughter burst amain
To see their children vainly strive and strive again.

V.

" Ill brooked fierce Tane to be thus defied ;
 So planting firm his head 'gainst Papa's breast,
And forcing open Rangi's inner side,
 His monstrous feet 'gainst his vast bulk he pressed,
And heaved and strove, and writhed as one distressed ;
 Still forcing Rangi high and Papa low,
Till streams of light gushed in from East to West,
 And darkness fled before her conquering foe :
The startled parents groaned, torn by the unnatural throe.

VI.

"'O shameful child,' they cried, 'O impious deed !
  To rend your guiltless parents thus in twain !'
But, spite of their reproach, did he proceed
  To thrust with feet, with giant back to strain—
Till they were cleft for good, nor met again.
  Lo ! children multitudinous now seen,
Which long concealed on Papa's breast had lain !
  Full strange seemed light and liberty, I ween,
To those who in such chaos dark confined had been.

VII.

"For aye those parents mourn this parting ; see
  How Papa lifts full oft her tear-stained veil,
And heaves and groans as though in misery ;
  And Rangi's answering eyelids never fail
To weep or softer rain, or bitterer hail,
  As moved by tenderness or passion more ;
Nought e'en doth soothing night's return avail
  To still his weeping ; for on Papa's floor
Each stilly morn he sheds his dewdrops—plenteous store.

VIII.

" Now Tawhiri-ma-tea, lord of blasts,
  His rage against his brothers ne'er forgets ;
E'en to this day his savage fury lasts :
  'Gainst Tane most, the lord of trees, he frets,
Who did the deed, the impious deed ; nor lets
  His vengeance sleep for his rent parents' sakes,
But for their severance nursing fond regrets,
  With gathered forces Tane's forest shakes,
Till, tottering to its roots, each woodland giant quakes.

IX.

"Next Tangaroa, lord of ocean, hears
    The wild wind's roaring, and the forest's crash,
And straight through all his watery realm he fears,
    And justly, for anon with furious dash
Swoops down Tawhiri, and his waves doth lash
    To sudden madness ; threatening ridges lift
Their crested tops, as though to quench the flash
    Of Rangi's stars ; meanwhile with fearsome rift
He tears old Ocean's floor, his very sands to shift.

X.

"While Tawhiri his vengeance thus pursued,
    Light was increased, and beings multiplied,
Not all like man, nor all unlike, but rude
    And monstrous forms : he who alone defied
Tawhiri's rage with stubborn, quenchless pride,
    Tumatauenga, he begat a race,
Which dwelt in caves, and roamed in forests wide,
    And wrought great change on Papa's rugged face,
Men to whom now our chiefs are proud their birth to trace.

XI.

"Much could I tell of Maui, wizard child,
    Of birth mysterious, cradled 'mid the foam
In seaweed tangles ; how by suasion mild
    He found a mother, and acquired a home ;
How vanished she each night, and back did come
    Each morn, until the boy her secret found :
How watching by the verge of heaven's dome,
    He and his brothers, for the rustling sound
Of the Sun's rising, dragged him headlong to the ground ;

XII.

"Snared him in noose prepared, then dragged him
        down ;
    And Maui wounded him, that he might go
Thenceforth more slowly, and the seasons crown
    With richer fruits.   'Twas Maui, you must know,
Who, with his brothers fishing once, did throw
    His magic hook into the fruitful sea,
And fished New Zealand from her bed below :
    Long time they tugged to haul the Island free,
Making its face so rough and mountainous to see.

XIII.

"Tawhaki too is famed in legends weird
    Whom kinsmen buried, thinking they had slain ;
But up he rose, and on a mountain reared
    A stronghold with his warriors.   Not in vain
He planned revenge, and sent down floods of rain
    To drown the guilty race.   A heavenly maid
Named Tango, smit with love, did not disdain
    To visit him ; for love she with him stayed,
Her friends forsook ; on earth for love her dwelling made—

XIV.

" Until he scorned her infant ; then she fled,
    And with her took the babe, and left him sad ;
' Come back, come back,' he cried—as overhead
    Her foot upon the roof she planted had
In act of leaving—' once more make me glad—
    I cannot live without thee : ' but she spurned
The roof and his entreaty, left him mad
    With vain remorse, and, as his spirit burned
With fierce despair, her pity kindled, and she turned,

C

XV.

"And, flying, cried, ' Farewell, and shouldst thou long
 To climb aloft, consumed by wasting love—
There is a certain place where creepers strong
 Hang down wind-wafted tendrils from above :
Beware you choose not such as loosely move
 Unfastened ; those alone, that touching cling
To earth and mount again will steadfast prove ;
 Once mounted, onward press, and love will bring
Thee where thy loved ones are, and every lovely thing.'

XVI.

"One moon he tarried ; then, o'erwhelmed with grief,
 Called to his brother Arihi, and said,
' Alas ! my brother, haste to my relief ;
 Come, seek with me my wife, who is not dead,
But dwelling in that country overhead ;
 For here since she is gone, I cannot stay '—
Then told the track which to that country led.
 They followed onward the directed way,
To where along the ground the pendant tendrils lay.

XVII.

" But Arihi forgat the warning voice,
 And rashly grasped a bough that loosely hung,
And bitter reason had to rue his choice ;
 For straight to the horizon he was flung
By a fierce hurricane, that sudden sprung :
 Ah ! that he might again touch earth ! But, no !
With equal force by backward gale he swung,
 Still tightly holding, dreading to let go—
Backwards and forwards, hither, thither, to and fro—

XVIII.

"At length brief respite, and on earth he leapt :
  Tawhaki, who had watched him with amaze,
Said, 'Brother, much I feared I should have wept
  Thy fatal fall ; now homewards go thy ways ;
Leave me to climb alone, Tawhaki prays.'
  With that he grasped a branch that firmly clung,
And, climbing up and up for many days,
  Reached the dear land ne'er told by mortal tongue,
And saw the blissful throngs his loved ones dwelt among.

XIX.

"By magic art assumed he strange disguise ;
  Seemed he a worn-out slave, crook-backed and old :
They made him bear their burdens ; in this wise
  He durst explore with secret steps yet bold
Each innermost recess, each hidden fold
  Of hill and glen, each dwelling great and small,
Hearkening meanwhile what one to other told,
  Until he reached a lofty, spacious hall,
Where dwelt those precious ones, to him were all in all.

XX.

"Judge ye his joy when first he saw the two,
  Mother and child ! Yet he his joy concealed,
Until occasion served ; then, breaking through
  His brief disguise, he straightway stood revealed
Resplendent, glorious, like a king annealed,
  As I have heard you speak of David's son :
He clasped his child ! Then sudden thunders pealed,
  And lightnings, flashing from his armpits, run
Through that adoring realm :—Kind Sirs, my tale is done."

XXI.

"The tales thou tellest, friend, are passing strange,"
    The Chaplain said, "yet mixed with twilight gleams
Of heavenly truth ; in earth's remotest range,
    From Arctic snows to India's fiercest beams,
Trace we dispersed and fragmentary streams
    From Revelation's source ; tales fanciful,
Such as thou tellest, like most other dreams,
    Not baseless are ; we from their store may cull
Lessons of wisdom true, as from a parable.

XXII.

"And list ye well, my missionary friends ;
    Scorn not such fables utterly, but sift
The grain from out the chaff ; your teaching tends
    To give new point to truth, when you can lift
Familiar legends to a higher drift :
    It wins men's hearts withal, to recognize
Traits of their native land ; the heavenly gift
    Of sympathy they hail, and fondly prize ;
See ! kindling interest awakes in answering eyes.

XXIII.

"Witness that cry for light : have we not read
    How in the primal days, ere man was made,
The world by darkness gross, was overspread ?
    How, when the solid firmament was laid,
The ancient elemental war was stayed ?
    But all by God's own Word ; here from the right
The ancestral legends of that land have strayed :
    'Twas at His Word that darkness took its flight :
'Let there be Light,' God said, and forthwith THERE WAS
    LIGHT.

XXIV.

"And in that monstrous brood, that raged so wild,
　　Rangi and Papa's sons, who does not see
The folk that lived before the Flood, defiled
　　With violence and savage cruelty,
Whose wickedness and foul iniquity,
　　Brought in the Flood upon that godless race,
Doomed to extermination utterly,
　　Save for a remnant spared·by God's mere grace?
From this Tawhaki's Flood its origin may trace.

XXV.

"Weird Maui's acts suggest to you to teach
　　That power o'er nature may indeed be won,
And works stupendous lie within our reach;
　　Yet not by sudden force must they be done,
As Maui snared and maimed the mighty Sun;
　　To knowledge, patient industry, and skill—
To those who humbly seek, not rashly run—
　　Doth nature yield her secrets: woo her still,
And she will still comply, nor ever work thee ill.

XXVI.

"Tawhaki's story soars to loftier height;
　　Shows heavenly wisdom come to dwell with man;
But, when he scorned her gift, she took her flight;
　　Yet left him not devoid of hope or plan,
But taught him how to follow, how to scan
　　Right warily the hopes on which to lean,
Trust no vain reeds, but mainstays such as can
　　Resist each threatening wind, sure bonds between
The changeless heaven and this aye-shifting earthly scene.

XXVII.

"'Grasp firm,' she said, 'a bough that comes from
    heaven,
    And taking root in earth, springs up again.'
Now one such Branch alone to us is given,
    The Lord that doth o'er all creation reign,
Who, taking all that doth to man pertain,
    Save only sin, struck root in earthly soil,
Then rose again to heaven, His own domain.
    Cling fast to Him, and, from this mortal coil
Released, you shall mount up where ends all care and toil.

XXVIII.

"Their fathers knew Him not, but they shall know,
    And teach their sons; His heralds through the land
The Gospel-trump ere long shall loudly blow,
    And news of peace shall spread on every hand,
Peace and goodwill to man; the saintly band
    Labours untold and perils shall endure
To win the land for Christ. Soon, as the sand
    Shall be their converts, and their victory sure;
For superstitions vile shall yield, and rites impure.

XXIX.

"My soul foresees a future for those Isles
    Of wondrous greatness—greatness, not of war,
But peaceful progress; lo! in thought defiles
    In long perspective, stretching out afar,
A bright array—Religion's guiding star,
    Trophies of Commerce, fruits of Industry;
Then sober Science, Art's triumphal car,
    Display of Mineral wealth, Thrift, Husbandry;
And, soaring ever higher, sweet Philosophy.

XXX.

" Not always shall the march be uniform ;
   Nor shall Religion always lead the van ;
Peace shall not always reign ; a scowling storm
   Shall sometimes rend the heavens. 'Tis not in man
To keep unerring, through the ages' span,
   The paths of truth and right. Depression may
Alternate with success. This only can
   Sustain the sinking heart—to work and pray,
Stand firm for God and Christ, and trust Him though He
   slay.

XXXI.

" All will work round with time. Let patience keep
   The Christian soul unmoved. God's work is slow,
As men count slowness, but is calm and deep :
   All will work round with time ; the wily foe
Has power to vex and thwart, and work men woe,
   But for a time, and for their final good :
The wheat and tares must aye together grow ;
   But wait the harvest ; ill, by faith withstood
Shall vanish, and God's plan at length be understood.

XXXII.

" Then shall shine forth the reign of righteousness,
   When crime and fraud and violence shall cease ;
Christ's living Presence shall His people bless,
   And Love walk hand in hand with meek-eyed Peace ;
Of growth of knowledge and of Joy's increase
   Shall be no pause ; to Christ all knees shall bend,
Who suffered on the Cross for man's release ;
   Glory and praise to Him shall aye ascend,
Father supreme Who reigns o'er all, world without end."

XXXIII.

A shade of awe o'erspread his manly face,
    As thus he spake : to Ruatara then
He turned and said, "But whence, my friend, thy race?
    How came they to that land so fair?   And when?"
"You must go back twice generations ten,"
    He said, "and to Hawaiki; thence we came :
In days of old that Island teemed with men ;
    But strife broke out, and, led by chiefs of name,
Our fathers sought new homes ; enshrined in deathless fame.

XXXIV.

"The memories of those leaders stand for aye—
    Chieftains thirteen, each o'er his own canoe :
Right nobly sped they, steering night and day,
    By sun and stars, full half a summer through
Toiling in rowing ; lo! each gallant crew
    A tribe's forefathers ; on the ocean wave
A floating nation ; wives and children too."
    "Thanks be to God," cried Marsden, "Who did save
Those brave ones in such peril from a watery grave!

XXXV.

"Saved them, I trow, for nobler things to come ;
    Thy teeming tribes, O friend, a time await,
When art, industrial skill, the total sum
    Of civilizing influences great,
Shall join with true religion to create
    The wonder of the Southern Hemisphere,
A sight magnificent to contemplate,
    A nation trained through self-respect to rear
Its cultured front, by gradual steps emerging clear.

XXXVI.

" From barbarous feuds and internecine strife,
 And horrid feasts of human flesh and gore,
To peaceful contests of a civil life,
 To reverence for law unknown before,
To love of learning, and to hopes that soar
 To higher worlds. Doubtless the bough long bent
Takes long to straighten. But the opened door
 Shall nevermore be closed. Our friends are sent,
Two brave fore-runners of a gallant armament,

XXXVII.

" Who shall instruct thy people in the way
 Of peace, and righteousness, and industry.
Thyself, O Ruatara, must essay
 Thy power, to civilize and mollify
Thy wild compatriots, that they may fly
 Like doves unto the windows of the ark.
Arouse thee, friend ; on this high destiny
 With gracious voice God calls thee to embark,
To be the first to raise thy land from ignorance dark."

XXXVIII.

He rose and paced the deck, rapt in high thought ;
 Then cried, uplifting earnest eyes above,
" O Thou, Great Lord, Who hast all nations bought
 With Thy dear blood, send down Thy Holy Dove
To wake those savage souls to answering love,
 And take from them a people for Thy name :
And give Thy grace to this young chief to move
 And change his people's hearts, their pride to tame,
And teach their lips glad songs of prayer and praise to
  frame."

XXXIX.

Then, with far-seeking eyes, and wondering gaze,
　He scanned the future, as some skipper pores
Over his charts, and through the thickening haze
　Peers into distance, blending far-off shores
With cloud-banks vague.   His ardent spirit soars
　To swift imagination's utmost bounds,
And rapt with sudden ecstasy, outpours
　Words gushing, as warm springs from hidden grounds,
Refusing utterance save in these poetic sounds :—

I.

Pride of the Australasian wave,
　Bright land of lovely sunset skies,
Fain would I search thine aspect grave,
　And solve thy hidden mysteries.

II.

Could sympathy thy heart unlock,
　And fervent love thy secrets win,
Soon would I rifle all thy stock,
　The lore thou treasurest up within.

III.

Two lots divide thy choice, fair land !
　Two paths outstretched before thee lie—
To seek thy good from others' hand,
　Or carve thine own high destiny.

IV.

Could I exert a potent voice,
   And patriotic fire instil,
I would infuse the nobler choice,
   Would rouse thy heart and nerve thy will.

V.

But patient must thou be, and learn :
   Slow grows the tree, slowly the child
Ripens to man ; so slowly turn
   A people's ways to soft from wild.

VI.

Let " Progress " be thy watchword : slow
   Or fast—what matters?   Onward aye !
Cease not, nor rest, but forward go,
   As run thy rivers night and day.

VII.

But wouldst thou rise to true renown,
   And purge thee from thy native dross,
'Mid nations win a glorious crown?
   Embrace, fair land, the Christian's Cross.

VIII.

The Cross will civilize the rude,
   Subdue the fierce, arouse the cold ;
Will charm thy savage multitude
   Into a meek, obedient fold.

IX.

Come quickly, Lord, with grace and power:
   Ancient of Days! Thine arm make bare,
And hasten the appointed hour,
   When one united cry of pray'r

X.

To Thee shall rise from every shore—
   To Thee accordant nations raise,
Loud as the mighty ocean's roar,
   Triumphant psalms of swelling praise.

Canto IV.

A GREAT VENTURE.

I.

O LAND of our adoption! Wert thou still,
　　As thou wert once, the sanguinary scene
Of homicidal rage—if Satan's will
　　Still mastered thy wild tribes—thou hadst not been
The home of Englishmen, whose flocks are seen
　　Fearlessly grazing on thy wolds ; thy coast
Not for inhospitable rocks, I ween,
　　Would have been shunned, but for thy savage host,
Of all the dreaded foes of light once dreaded most.

II.

O ye who dwell at ease on hill or plain,
　　Or by the salt sea-wave, to whom the lines
Have fallen in pleasant places, or whom gain
　　Tempts by the hoarded riches of our mines ;
Ye merchants, statesmen, scholars, and divines,
　　Remember aye your debt to those who led,
And those who fostered, the sublime designs
　　Of Mission zeal, by self-devotion fed,
Sustained by patience, and with calm discretion wed.

III.

Of patience and discretion was there need :
    Years intervened, for terror caused delay :
O ! horrid name of " Boyd !"   O frightful deed
    With that sad name allied !   Oh ! fearsome day ! *
A fair ship in the Bay of Islands lay :
    A native chief had shipped among her crew :
Him had the skipper outraged, so they say,
    By cruel floggings ; thirst for vengeance grew ;
His tribesmen gathered, seized their time, arose and slew—

IV.

Threescore and ten they slew ; they slew and ate—
    Seamen and passengers ; but two they spared.
Long was it ere that horror did abate :
    Marsden himself, whose dauntless soul had dared
To face the worst, regardless how he fared,
    Yearned for the high emprise, but rashness feared :
    Careless of self, for others' safety cared.
    High mountains thus their icy barriers reared,
Yet faith's strong prayer at length the chilling prospect
    cleared.

---

* "*After their arrival at Sydney, in February, 1810, Ruatara was Mr. Marsden's guest for some months, during which he applied himself eagerly to agriculture, and the acquirement of other useful knowledge, his one absorbing desire being to benefit his countrymen. Then, impelled by a love of home, he took advantage of an opportunity of returning to the Bay of Islands, and the two catechists were to have accompanied him ; but just at that time tidings reached Sydney of what is known as " the Massacre of the Boyd," at the harbour of Whangaroa, which lies some distance to the north of the Bay of Islands, a fearful act of revenge taken by the natives for indignities suffered by one of their chiefs at the hands of the captain of that vessel, similar to those Ruatara had endured, and which involved, not only the burning of the ship, but the massacre of the crew and passengers, amounting to nearly seventy persons, eight only having escaped. The general horror caused by this event was greatly increased by the 'o'er true tale' of cannibalism connected with it."—" Colonial Church Histories : New Zealand :" by the Very Rev. H. Jacobs, page 9.*

V.

Time rested not ; four years had passed and more
  Since those devoted comrades, King and Hall,
Had trodden first Australia's golden shore :
  Meanwhile, O God, Who know'st the hearts of all,
Whose grace alone can shield men lest they fall,
  Who triest human souls as gold is tried,
Thou didst from England Thomas Kendall call.*
  Then to those three heroic Marsden cried,
" Up, tarry we no longer, nor unmoved abide,

VI.

"While Satan reigns in triumph. Up, my friends,
  'Tis time to make the venture. Trust in Him,
Who needful help His trusting servants sends :
  Our Mission brig, the " Active," stout and trim,
Awaits you in yon port ; with prayer and hymn
  We send you forth, Kendall and William Hall,
The Saviour's heralds, to a future dim,
  Yet hopeful : let your God be all in all ;
Christ guide you, bless you, comfort you, whate'er befall.

VII.

" Go now as pioneers to smooth the way,
  With Ruatara friendship to renew ;
Greet him with kind remembrances, and say
  We look to him for aid ; if he but knew
The longing of our hearts his land to view,
  And win his people to the arts of peace,
His zeal would quick revive. We know him true,
  Believe him constant : bid him never cease
From his old patriot fire, his ardour to release

---

* Subsequent events proved that there was grave reason for distrusting the sincerity
and uprightness of this person, who was ultimately " disconnected " from their service
by the C.M.S. See " Colonial Church Histories : New Zealand," pages 28-31, 34, 37.

VIII.

"His people from their Foe." They went and came,
 Ere many moons their rapid course had run—
So well the "Active" justified her name—
 To where beneath New Zealand's kindly sun
Young Ruatara had his work begun—
 And back to Sydney. He had sown the grain
Of glorious wheat, no Maori yet had done ;
 The golden ears had gathered, and would fain
Have ground them into flour, but strove and strove in vain.

IX.

But now what joy their coming would afford !
 How good a thoughtful gift in hour of need !
Marsden, this need foreseeing, placed on board
 The Brig a hand-mill. From his trouble freed,
The grateful Ruatara blessed the deed,
 And blessed the giver. Changed the scene ere long ;
For back to Sydney did the young chief speed ;
 With him his uncle Hongi, and a throng
Of eager native chiefs, with names unmeet for song.

X.

How shall I picture Hongi ? Gruesome chief !
 What deeds of blood he nurtured in his heart !
What deeds of wild ambition past belief !
 Yet he concealed them with the subtlest art
Beneath a guise of gentleness. Some part
 Of the true hero bore he 'neath the veil ;
High-souled, he could forgive, forbear, impart
 To others of his own ; full oft a tale
Of shameful wrong to rouse his anger might prevail.

XI.

And now in sooth the mission life began :
    Hall, Kendall, King, with wives and children sailed
On board the " Active," and that dauntless man,
    Marsden, their head : not for one moment quailed
That heaven-sustained spirit ; else had failed
    That life-fraught enterprise.   A gallant friend,
Hight Nicholas,* whose manly cheek ne'er paled
    At shock of danger, and eight Maories bend
Their course to Rangihoua, timely help to lend ;

XII.

To Rangihoua, Ruatara's home :
    But first to Whangaroa's bay they steer,
With hearts courageous, o'er the ocean's foam ;
    And courage, if at all, was needed here ;
For here lay fragments, scattered far and near,
    Of the ill-fated " Boyd ; " that outrage dire
Might well have shook the stoutest heart with fear,
    When savage fury loosed the bands of fire,
And glutted to the full its homicidal ire.

XIII.

Wisely he aimed their confidence to gain
    By fearless frankness and by loving trust,
Hoping they would repay—nor hoped in vain—
    His proffered friendship with requital just.
Who would win access to the heathen, must
    Approach them thus with outstretched arms of love ;
Alas ! when deeds of avarice and lust
    The true descent of mis-named Christians prove,
And in untutored hearts not love but madness move.

* *This gentleman, on his return to England, published a " Narrative of a Voyage
to New Zealand" in two volumes. (Black, 1817.)*

D

XIV.

The Whangaroans and the Mission's friends
    Were waging deadly feud; and for the sake
Of holy peace, and for the sacred ends
    Of the great work he toiled for, and to make
Their outlook tranquil, Marsden strove to break
    The cruel rancour of that enmity;
So went ashore unarmed, nor would he take
    For retinue a greater company
Than seven, that all his peaceful aim might plainly see.

XV.

But ne'er did conqu'ror with sublimer tread
    Descend upon a foreign shore, nor king
Advance with more assurance at the head
    Of loyal followers his land to bring
To seek return to favour 'neath his wing:
    With nobler courage Cæsar did not land
On Albion's Isle, nor Norman William fling
    His prostrate form upon our Sussex strand,
Clasping more eagerly to heart the mother-sand.

XVI.

But not, like theirs, self-seeking was his aim,
    That captive princes might his triumph grace;
Not for vain-glory, nor the patriot's fame;
    But that that sinful folk might seek the face
Of God, and live; that a benighted race
    Might find deliverance and joy and light.
Can we not here a loftier glory trace?
    Not self, but Christ; by spirit, not by might:
By meekness, not by force; by faith, and not by sight.

XVII.

They went on shore, I said ; and on the cliff
  The natives stood, drawn up in armed array :
Marsden, unmoved by this reception stiff,
  Clomb with his friends to face them, bold as they,
And thus by an interpreter 'gan say :—
  "We come to you, my brothers, in the Name
Of Him, Who rules the darkness and the day,
  Almighty God, Who made this earthly frame,
And all mankind. We come to teach His righteous way.

XVIII.

"I am no stranger ; you have heard of me ;
  And many of your countrymen I know :
Trust me ; for I have come across the sea
  With no intent but seeds of love to sow ;
To open doors of knowledge, and to show
  How all your lives may pure and happy be ;
How, day by day, may purer, happier, grow.
  We come from fear of death to set you free,
And wrest from man's dread conqueror his victory.

XIX.

"We come not now to see you and depart,
  But, some of us, to sojourn months and years :
And I entreat you, brethren, on your part,
  That they may dwell among you free from fears :
Nay, I implore you earnestly with tears,
  That you will lay aside your enmity,
Whate'er its origin, with your compeers,
  Your warlike neighbours in the Bay hard by :
Kinsmen should be at peace, and cease from rivalry."

XX.

With dovelike sweetness, but undaunted mien
   Thus spake he ; and, as oil outpoured on wave
Smoothes the rough surface of the turbid scene,
   So those wild men, erstwhile so sternly grave,
Relaxed the fierceness hostile fury gave
   To every feature ; as soft breezes melt
The bitterest frosts, so words of kindness drave
   Their wrath away ; so surely kindness dealt
Wakes in unhardened hearts return of kindness felt.

XXI.

That night he slept among them with his friends,
   A motley group upon the natural ground ;
No hut o'erhead, nor tent its covering lends ;
   No guard ; no camp-fire lit to circle round ;
The balmy air ensures their slumbers sound ;
   The warriors' spears stood up amid the fern
Erect like sentinels ; the skies star-crowned
   That lustrous night did so intensely burn,
They seemed with fondly, loving zeal o'er men to yearn.

XXII.

The rippling wave so gently kissed the shore,
   As murmuring to the sleepers on the hill
Of home and children. What could nature more
   To whisper rest? Yet Marsden slept but ill ;
So strangely was he moved, such thoughts would fill
   His heart, as he surveyed the marv'llous scene ;
And as he pondered the adventure, still
   Awe and amazement grew : for ne'er, I ween,
Was in this earthly life more strange conjuncture seen.

XXIII.

Five years had scarce elapsed since English blood
    Imbrued those vengeful hands; now calmly slept
Around him, o'er whose souls a whelming flood
    Of furious passion then unbridled swept:
All now so tranquil! He had well-nigh wept
    To think how blest the contrast. Might it be
A heaven-sent omen? How his spirit leapt
    With joy such forecast of sweet peace to see—
Two races blent as one in Christian unity.

XXIV.

Next morn they woke as comrades sworn of old,
    And noisy salutations met his ear,*
Tena-koe, from voices manifold,
    And *Haere-mai:* then said he, "Comrades dear,
Come, board with me my vessel; what good cheer
    I have, is yours: partake our morning meal."
They trusted him, and laid aside all fear:
    Thus mutual confidence can festers heal,
And that which boded woe, can turn to lasting weal.

XXV.

Their wayward spirits further he subdued
    By well-judged presents; then with earnest prayer
Implored them to forego their long-nursed feud.
    And oh! what joy! what peace-maker would dare
To hope so soon such reconcilement rare?
    With Ruatara and with Hongi they
Join hand in hand, and to give proof they bare
    No malice still—laugh not, I pray—they lay
Their noses side by side—such is their nation's way.†

* "Tenakoe" is equivalent to "How do you do?" literally it means, "That you," or, "There you are." "Haere-mai" is literally, "Come hither," and is the ordinary salutation of "Welcome."

† "Rubbing noses," as it is termed by the English, is the ordinary mutual salutation of the Maori race.

XXVI.

Nor will they hurt the trader—so they vow—
    And will protect the Missioners from harm.
" Now blest be God ! our heads shall thankful bow
    To Him Who hath stretched forth His mighty arm
To shield our lives from peril and alarm "—
    Did Marsden awestruck piously exclaim—
" And hath o'er this fine people cast the charm
    Of soul-subduing grace ; may He reclaim
Their souls from sin and Satan through Christ's holy Name."

XXVII.

And now drew near the blessed, glorious time
    Of the dear Saviour's birth, the bright, glad Day
We Christians celebrate in every clime,
    In frigid zone, or 'neath the torrid ray,
From callow youth until our beards grow grey :
    This year it fell on Sunday ; thus full well
The time was suited in a twofold way
    For the first Christian Service ; who can tell
How solemn the event that on that day befell ?*

XXVIII.

At Rangihoua was the chosen spot :
    There Ruatara had prepared the ground :
Canoes to seat the English he had got ;
    His folk on mother earth would squat around.
A flagstaff he had raised upon a mound,
    Whence Marsden from the deck, that Christmas
        morn—
And oh ! what joy did in his heart abound,
    Joy of enthusiastic forecast born !—
Beheld our English flag that land of hope adorn.

* A.D. 1814. By a happy coincidence that Christmas-Day was also a Sunday.

XXIX.

"Float blithely on the breeze," the Chaplain cried,
　"Bright augury of happier days to be!
Glad sign of freedom! spread thee far and wide;
　Proclaim abroad a glorious liberty
From Satan's thraldom; Jesus sets men free,
　The Lord of life and glory, born this day:
Waft, waft the message over land and sea,
　Till every heart shall learn the angel lay,
'Peace and goodwill to man, glory to God for aye.'"

XXX.

He came ashore, and oh! how strange the scene!
　The chiefs their men had marshalled in array;
Not, as of yore, for clash of arms, I ween,
　Not to yell threats, nor bid them up and slay;
But to precede them in a better way:
　When Marsden came, they led them to the spot,
The holy spot, where he should kneel and pray:
　Hushed was the expectation and intense,
And breathless silence held them rapt in chained suspense.

XXXI.

The grand Old Hundredth first they sang aloud;
　The Prayers then read he, Psalms and Lessons too;
All heads meanwhile were reverently bowed:
　Hushed was the awe, deep the devotion grew:
Pierced was he to the depths, and stricken through
　With strong emotion, as he thought how strange
Their inward musings; though his message new
　They understood not, yet a loftier range
Their hearts would gain, and conscious be of hidden change.

XXXII.

" Glad tidings of great joy to you I bring "—
  Such was his text ; and sure no fitter verse
Could claim his choice.   With what a glorious ring
  It sounded o'er that coast, and bade disperse
Dense clouds of ignorance, and darkness worse
  Than that Egyptian ! Then did he proclaim
JESUS, the Son of God, sent to reverse
  The general doom—the Virgin-born Who came
To raise mankind to life by power of His dear Name.

XXXIII.

Oh ! what a glorious day, whereon was lit
  A beacon on New Zealand's topmost height
Shall nevermore expire ; whereon was writ
  The opening chapter of a tale so bright !
Lord ! shed thereon an ever-brightening light !—
  "The History of New Zealand's Church !" O thou,
First of those worthies, whose pure record white
  Maketh her annals lustrous, on thy brow
We place a wreath the sternest justice will allow.*

XXXIV.

For in this century no work more grand
  Shines forth than his ; a barbarous race reclaimed
From horrid superstitions doth command
  Our ceaseless admiration—made ashamed
Of its own vileness, sick at heart, self-blamed,
  Crying heart-deep with inarticulate cry
For light and purity ; its fierceness tamed :
  Know'st thou within the range of history
Such transformation wrought by Christianity ?

---

* The writer remembers to have heard Bishop Selwyn several times, both in public
and private, emphatically ascribe the honour of evangelizing the natives of New
Zealand to Samuel Marsden.

XXXV.

But, gentles, list ye ; I would fain invite
    Your loving interest in this my lay,
The while a tale of pathos I recite,
    Which, were it told you in a worthier way,
Would grieve, yet charm you all the livelong day.
    Poor Ruatara, child of many a storm,
Sheltered at length, it seemed, in his own bay—
    Poor hunted stag, around whose prostrate form
Misfortune's ruthless pack full oft did howling swarm —

XXXVI.

True patriot he, on many a sage design
    He ruminated for his people's good,
And for the Mission ; here, by rule and line
    A town he would construct ; well understood
He measure and proportion ; thus he would
    His streets lay out, and here a market wide ;
Here build a church with tapering spire of wood :
    But, ere the " Active " sailed, alas ! the tide
Of his brief life ran out, he sickened, pined, and died.

XXXVII.

Ask you how fared his soul in that dread strife ?
    Not clear his faith—ah ! no ! nor stayed his mind
By sure and certain hope of endless life :
    Dark were his thoughts, alas ! his judgment blind :
Close-clinging superstitions did enwind
    Around his spirit struggling to be free—
Struggling, as oft against the stormy wind
    And murky tempest battling o'er the lea,
Few sunbeams quickly vanquished you may sadly see.

XXXVIII.

Yet say not all was dark ; within that breast
  Were eager aspirations after light :
That very agitation and unrest
  Betoken noble longings for the right.
A native sorcerer priest with hellish might
  Withstood those yearnings : help, O Christ, we pray,
That fine, heroic soul, and speed its flight
  To where—oh ! may it be !—some brightening ray
May light its gloom : bring Thou, Oh ! bring him to the Day!

XXXIX.

Saddest of all and strange beyond belief !
  This kingly man unwittingly betrayed,
To Marsden's deep astonishment and grief,
  Grave doubts, which half unconsciously had preyed
Long time upon his inmost soul, and weighed
  Him down with gloom—doubts lest that high emprise
Would prove his country's bane, a paving laid
  For subjugation, a contrivance wise
To steal their freedom 'neath religion's holy guise.

XL.

Whence came this whisper, Marsden guessed in vain,
  Save that he knew it artfully inspired
By crafty foes, laying insidious train
  Of venomous aspersions : one so fired
With love of country, who to plans aspired
  And deeds magnanimous, thus took alarm :
Imbibed the poison quickly as desired :
  "See to *Australia's* folk the deadly harm,
By England wrought," they said, "and dread the fatal
    charm."

XLI.

When death drew nigh, they bore him to the hill
　　" Te Puna," or " The Spring," where he might die ;
Since within doors to die, foreboded ill ;
　　Here, where he had thought to build on high
His town, here he his latest breath did sigh :
　　Pathetic close of a pathetic life ;
Nor ended even thus its tragedy :
　　Plunged in despair, o'erwhelmed with grief, his wife
By her own hands for ever closed her mortal strife.

XLII.

While yet he lay a-dying, Marsden sailed,
　　With mingled feelings parting from his friends ;
His watchful love not for one moment failed ;
　　He knew their danger ; but his fervour lends
Its own contagion to their hearts, and tends
　　To lift them with enthusiastic zeal
Above all fear ; and now my canto ends :
　　These parting words his sympathy reveal,
Ere on the shore with prayer their last farewells they seal.

HYMN OF THANKSGIVING.

I.

Thanks, thanks to God ! the glorious work's begun :
　　Grant it may never cease !
The heavenly news throughout the centuries run,
　　Glory, goodwill, and peace !

II.

Angels, rejoice !   Behold a race new-born ;
  Behold new light arisen
To gladden with a bright and joyous morn
  The tenants of a prison !

III.

Thousands shall rise from out this favoured land
  To bless His glorious Name,
Who knits by faith and love the saintly band,
  And keeps them through the same.

IV.

Brave gentleness and manly purity
  Shall many a life adorn :
Not on their face alone shall sanctity,
  But in their hearts, be worn.

V.

With high resolves, great aims, yet childlike trust
  Shall many a heart be filled :
Hope of the resurrection of the just
  Shall many a death-bed gild.

VI.

So gird you bravely to your task, dear friends ;
  Quit you like men, be strong :
In needful hour, when prayer to heaven ascends,
  Due succour waits not long.

VII.

To this grand work God calls us from on high ;
    The Church looks on with awe :
The scattered Isles beneath the jewelled sky
    Are waiting for His law.

VIII.

With courage then and patience bear your parts :
    Let dangers ne'er oppress :
Nor persecutions vex you, but your hearts
    Let God's own peace possess.

IX.

Now to the Father's watchful care, my friends,
    And to the Saviour's grace
My soul in sympathy your souls commends :
    The brightness of His face

X.

Shine all around you, and your spirits cheer
    With never-failing love !
The Holy Spirit's inward presence near
    Your constant succour prove !

Canto V.

BUILDING UP.

I.

How grandly pictured on Time's canvas stands
 The growing fabric of the Church of God ;
Built up of living stones, reared without hands,
 Through every race and nation spread abroad,
In every land by human footsteps trod,
 In silence growing with the growth of time,
Behold her towering high, extending broad !
 Holy, august, beneficent, sublime,
Fulfilling to the end the promise of her prime !

II.

Fair art thou, Sion ; thou dost cause to sing
 With joy the earth ; upon thy northern side
Lieth the City of the heavenly King,
 Which, on thy hill high-seated, nought can hide ;
Adorned with jewels as a royal bride ;
 Go round about her, mark her bulwarks well ;
Reckon her towers how high, her gates how wide ;
 Survey her palaces where angels dwell,
That to your sons to come her glories ye may tell.

III.

Most real are those g'ories, Sion blest :
　Thy walls salvation are ; thy gates are praise ;
Thy palaces a refuge for oppressed
　And weary souls ; thy towers their bulwarks raise
From Satan's wiles to shield us all our days :
　The jewels which the queenly Bride adorn
Are Faith, which guides her aye in holy ways,
　And Hope, which points her to the coming morn,
And Love, which, like her Lord, shews mercy to the lorn.

IV.

Thus Marsden mused, as from the Bay he sailed :
　Mused he how men of God in days of old,
Who trusted in His help, had never quailed,
　But, spite of hardships, trials manifold,
Of labours infinite, of strifes untold,
　To bear Christ's standard up did bravely dare ;
Their faith, though tried with fire, proved sterling gold :
　Such strength is theirs who, watching aye to prayer,
Straight to God's mercy-seat in needful hour repair.

V.

Musing he lay through half a summer night,
　And, as he mused, he half-unconscious grew :
Calmly, yet swiftly, borne by breezes light,
　The "Active" o'er the tranquil waters flew :
Through the slant port-hole lustrous moonbeams threw
　Their tremulous, tender gleams on all that hung
The cabin's precincts round, its chattels few,
　And books and pictures ; rustling murmurs sung
Low chants amid the shrouds, and hushed was every tongue.

VI.

The watch slow-pacing on the deck o'erhead,
　　The wave soft-rippling 'neath the gliding keel—
These sounds except, all else was still as dead—
　　When Marsden, lo! not sees, but seems to feel
A sudden presence; and, despite his zeal
　　And well-proved courage, an o'ermastering fear
Confounds his reason; for a moment reel
　　His dizzy senses, as though death stood near,
And grimly threatened, brandishing his dreadful spear.*

VII.

But God, Who ne'er His trusting ones forsakes,
　　Is aye at hand to soothe their natural fears;
So Marsden, as to consciousness he wakes,
　　These gentle, reassuring accents hears—
And as the words of comfort reach his ears,
　　A dazzling radiance all the cabin fills,
As of a star outshining all compeers—
　　The solemn Voice, while every nerve it thrills,
His throbbing bosom's discomposure quickly stills.

VIII.

'Twas thus It spake:—"To help thee, not to fright,
　　O Man of God, I come; therefore take heart;
Thy work is precious in the Father's sight;
　　Thou the Apostle of New Zealand art,
And I its Angel; thus a brother's part
　　I share with thee: transports of joy and praise
Burst forth in heavenly places at the start
　　Of thy great enterprise: in all thy ways
Be mine and theirs to watch and shield thee many days!

* I need scarcely say, that this vision is wholly imaginary.

IX.

"Great things hath God in store for that fair land ;
  And many saints, who shall hereafter rise,
Are hid as polished shafts in His right hand,
  Men gentle as the dove, as serpents wise."
Marsden, now fully roused, yet trembling, cries :
  "O holy one, I thank the gracious Lord
That He hath blessed His lowly servant's eyes
  With such bright vision, and hath sent His word
To gladden these dull ears : Oh ! speak ; I will afford

X.

"Devout attention ; who shall first arise
  To drive away the darkness, and to sound
The Gospel trumpet ?   May these longing eyes
  Behold God's husbandmen that untilled ground
With zealous toil subdue, and scatter round
  Seeds of eternal life !   I ask not all
The Missionary roll, but who shall found
  A Church in that new land, that ne'er shall fall,
Till God at last this guilty world to Judgment call ?"

XI.

"Be still, and hearken then," the Angel spake :
  "Not first in order, but in honour chief,
Shall Henry Williams for the Gospel's sake,
  To spread among that people the Belief,
Which slays the love of sin, and scatters grief—
  That Jesus died for men and rose again—
Spend and be spent, and offer the first sheaf
  Of souls redeemed—shall labour not in vain,
And, many hardships past, shall reap eternal gain.

E

XII.

"Soon shalt thou welcome him on Sydney's shore,
    Shrewd, enterprising, resolute, and brave :
Whilom in England's navy arms he bore,
    Learnt readiness and skill to stem the wave ;
Learnt the ripe knowledge such experience gave
    Of men and things, right precious store for aid
In Mission labours : He Who died to save
    Demands that every talent should be made
A willing sacrifice upon God's altar laid.

XIII.

" So shall not many months elapse, ere he
    Shall build a vessel in Paihia's Bay—
For those onlookers strange the sight to see !—
    Their needed stores from Sydney to convey,
And bear the Gospel o'er the watery way
    To neighbouring and to distant tribes ; her name
Shall fitly be the ' Herald '; on the day
    She shall be launched, so great shall be her fame
That years shall chronicle the chiefs who came *

XIV.

"To view the great event ; and oh ! what joy
    Shall signalize that schooner's first emprise !
What errand first shall his new craft employ ?
    What else but this—with loving, longing eyes
To greet his brother ? This long-hoped-for prize
    Waits him at Sydney. Fears he much to miss
His brother on the deep ; but glad surprise
    Shall bid the sudden tear to start, I wis,
When, landing on the quay, he meets a brother's kiss.

* The " Herald" was launched on the 24th January, 1826.

XV.

" Ah ! noble pair of brothers ! On the roll
   Of missionary heroes shall they stand
Pre-eminent, united as one soul :
   From their arrival on that favoured strand
Shall date the onward march throughout the land,
   Not in one corner only, but around—
North, South, and West—of the invading band,
   Till their word reach New Zealand's utmost bound,
And every valley echo as with trumpet-sound.*

XVI.

" First inward to Waimate shall they pass ;
   Then southward to the Thames their torch's light
'Midst cruel habitations, and alas !
   'Midst deeds of rapine, and the horrid sight
Of human feasts, shall strive with hellish night.
   Then to the Eastward Cape the ' Herald ' trim
Shall wing her way with joy-diffusing flight :
   Captives unchained their new-born bliss shall hymn ;
No hostile rage shall daunt, no scorn their courage dim.

XVII.

" Fresh labourers shall come to share the toil,
   And occupy fresh stations, two and two ;
Tauranga, and the steam-emitting soil
   Of Rotorua ; and Kaitaia too

---

* Archdeacons Henry and William Williams. The latter afterwards became the
first Bishop of Waiapu, A.D. 1859. For the lives of these two admirable men, see
" The Life of Henry Williams," by Hugh Carleton (his son-in-law). (Auckland: Upton
and Co., 1874.) " Christianity Among the New Zealanders," by the Right Rev. William
Williams, Bishop of Waiapu. (London, Seeley and Co., 54, Fleet Street, 1867.)
" Colonial Church Histories: New Zealand," (S.P.C.K., 1889), Part I.

Towards North Cape ; Mount Egmont's westward view,
    By fruitful Taranaki ; Taupo's Lake ;
The Stream that winds Waikato's valley through ;
    And fearsome Tarawera, who shall make
Sometime the neighbouring region far and wide to shake ;

XVIII.

" And lordly Tongariro, towering high ;
    The everlasting hills their voice shall hear
That publish peace : the lowly vales shall sigh
    With plaintive penitence and humble fear,
As though they heard their Lord ; the plains shall rear
    Their palms outspread in earnest, trustful pray'r ;
One tuneful note of adoration clear
    And thankful joy the rivers everywhere
By rock and fell shall to the Eternal Ocean bear.

XIX.

" God to those brothers shall give faithful wives,
    Meet helpmates of their missionary care,
Experienced mothers, whose wise, thoughtful lives
    Shall to those nature's waifs be patterns rare :
Their husbands' part shall be to do and dare,
    But theirs full oft to sadly wait and weep,
While tarries long the Mission-ship, and fare
    Those sailor-priests full roughly on the deep,
While hungry billows round them wildly howl and leap.*

---

* *See Carleton's " Life of Henry Williams"—passim. This is an intensely interesting book, the more so, as being the work of a layman, who is also a distinguished journalist and politician, as well as a scholar and a gentleman. See " Col. Ch. Hist.," p. 371. Mrs. Henry Williams died some years ago, but the widow of the first Bishop of Waiapu is still living at Napier, being upwards of ninety years of age.*

XX.

" O William Williams, great shall be thy fame
  For skill in mastering the Maori tongue ;
Nor shall that honour soon desert thy name :
  For Leonard Williams,* honoured e'en when young,
Told by historian and by poet sung,
  As sharing with his father the renown,
From skill, sagacity, and learning sprung,
  By grateful generations handed down,
A life of usefulness with endless bliss shall crown.

XXI.

" Yet Robert Maunsell shall their equal be : †
  In God's translated Word shall be his praise :
For ever honoured be his industry
  And fervent zeal !   In many crafty ways,
Crafty yet blameless, he shall spend his days
  In fuller, freer wise their speech to learn ;
Like a good steward, who his talent lays
  To good advantage out, and strives to turn
All to God's glory.   Such to their deep joy shall earn

XXII.

" That glorious meed, ' Well done, thou faithful one ! '
  And shall I tell of other faithful men ?—
Chapman, whose face shall beam as doth the sun,
  Whom natives shall call ' Happy man ; ' ‡ and then

---

* *The Ven. William Leonard Williams, B.A., Principal of the Theological College,
Gisborne, formerly of Magdalen Hall, now Hertford College, Oxford, to whom the See
of Waiapu was offered by the Synod of the Diocese after the resignation of his father
in 1876. See "Colonial Church Histories: New Zealand," page 383.*

† *Dr. (formerly Archdeacon) Maunsell, LL.D., Trinity College, Dublin, is still
living in an honoured old age at Parnell, Auckland. See "Colonial Church Histories:
New Zealand," (S.P.C.K.), page 127.*

‡ *" Hapimana" was their rendering of " Chapman"—a singularly happy mistake
in his case.*

Of Ashwell's fiery zeal and fervour, when
 Proclaiming Gospel truth, but loving mien
In friendly converse ; * and with subtle pen
 Hadfield acute and eloquent, between
Life and the sleep of death full often hovering seen.†

XXIII.

" Of priests in that fair land the first in date
 Shall Hadfield be ordained ; of Bishops too
To sees within New Zealand consecrate
 Shall he be first. Stands out in distant view
The Primacy, to lifelong labours due,
 And masterly superiority :
For men shall cherish that devotion true,
 That, when a Priest was sought, was heard to cry,
' Send me, a dying man ; what matters *where* we die ? ' ‡

XXIV.

" Those men of God shall yearn to stem the flood
 Of horrid war ; shall threats and perils dare,
To check the intertribal flow of blood ;
 With spirit dauntless and with courage rare
Shall visit hostile camps, nor efforts spare
 To cause the combatants their rage forsake :
And so the Prince of Peace, Who doth declare
 That Blessed are the Peacemakers, shall make
Those pastors by consent the place of umpires take.

* *The Rev. B. Y. Ashwell was, in the first instance, a missionary at Sierra Leone ; afterwards in the Lower Waikato, N.Z., and lastly, in 1868, held a cure at the North Shore, Auckland. His widow is still living at Parnell.*

† *Ordained priest by Bishop Broughton at Waimate in 1839, being the first clergyman ordained to the priesthood in New Zealand ; settled as missionary at Otaki in the October of that year ; appointed Archdeacon of Kapiti by Bishop Selwyn ; consecrated second Bishop of Wellington by Bishop Harper, Oct. 9th, 1870 ; elected Primate by the General Synod on Feb. 26th, 1889 ; resigned Primacy in May, 1893. With reference to Bishop Hadfield's frail health see Tucker's " Life and Episcopate of Bishop Selwyn," Vol. I., pp. 186, 187 ; " Colonial Church Histories : New Zealand," pp. 126, 127.*

‡ *See " Col. Ch. Hist. : New Zealand," p. 81.*

XXV.

"So now, where carnage fell and brutal rage
　　Once outraged heaven's fair face, there meek-eyed
　　　Peace
Shall rear a shrine, and soon the iron age
　　Shall brighten into silver : men shall cease
To hate and fear each other ; large increase
　　Of industry and knowledge shall succeed ;
Instead of robbing, men shall buy and lease :
　　Yet oh ! let them abhor the love of greed,
And fear lest peaceful commerce selfish cunning breed.

XXVI.

"But now a change draws near ; the time demands
　　More settled order, and the plan divine
Requires that now into a Bishop's hands
　　The reins of power be trusted ; but so fine
Are the adjustments of the grand design,
　　That wisdom from above, sagacity,
Firmness with sweetness, an exhaustless mine
　　Of love profound, and truest sympathy,
Are needed to maintain the heavenly harmony.

XXVII.

"And even such the grace that shall be given
　　To Selwyn, of New Zealand's prelates first :
As oft in mountain chain that neighbours heaven,
　　Some loftier peak is seen through clouds to burst,
And now again is hid, in gloom immersed,
　　Yet haply catches transient beams of light,
Defying threatening storms to rage their worst—
　　Through good report and ill, through dark and bright,
Strong and inflexible shall he uphold the right.

XXVIII.

" A very prince of men, and large of heart :
　　E'en those who love him not, must needs revere ;
But most shall love him, for his matchless art
　　Of winning those who deem him most severe :
But few shall shun his countenance through fear,
　　And those the worthless : the distressed, the weak,
The helpless and the lonely shall be dear
　　As his own flesh ; in his true kindness seek
Source of the tear that moistens many a widowed cheek.

XXIX.

" High works he shall attempt : in counsel great,
　　And wise to gather from each man his best ;
Patient for opportunities to wait ;
　　Well knowing when to urge, and when to rest ;
Fearless to meet, and resolute to breast
　　Each adverse tide, he shall behold the day,
Whereto he hath unceasing onward pressed,
　　When the Church fabric shall reposing stay,
Built on consenting Orders, Bishops, Clergy, Lay.

XXX.

" Wise counsellors shall gather round, and share
　　His lofty toil, men versed in holy page,
And trained to scrutinize with reverent care
　　The precedents of many a bygone age :
And chiefly William Martin, calmly sage,
　　With gentle mien and mild persuasive speech,
The hearts of listening Synods shall engage :
　　To future years his treasured words shall reach,
And to the unborn Church shall honeyed wisdom teach.

XXXI.

" One more dear name, the saintly Patteson,
      Shall evermore with Selwyn's be allied ;
As sacred charge bequeathed by sire to son,
      So shall that Mission be o'er ocean wide,
With those twin names for aye identified :
      Selwyn and Patteson, Selwyn again,
Loud shall proclaim the Name of Him Who died :
      Through isles that throng the Melanesian main,
Thick as the glittering gems that stud night's glorious train.

XXXII.

"And now commend I thee to His kind care
      Who made the heavens, in Whom both you and we
At every instant live and move and are :
      Be strong and fear not : He hath let thee see
The first leaves of a wondrous history,
      Thyself the frontispiece : as mothers yearn
Over a first-born babe, so tenderly
      Will I watch o'er thy work ; with such concern
For thy new Church, and fair New Zealand's honour burn."

XXXIII.

Faded the Vision from the Chaplain's sight,
      Yet left soft radiance in that cabin low,
As, when a good man dieth, calmly bright
      Doth linger, like the sunset's afterglow,
His memory's sweetness ; and his friends are slow
      To understand their loss, and scarce believe
His presence parted from them ; even so
      Would Marsden fain a fuller gift receive ;
So grudged he of that gracious One to take his leave.

XXXIV.

Yet, as the " Active" sped her homeward way,
 His heart beat gladly, and fresh courage took :
Then cried he, " Lord of heaven and earth, I pray,
 Hear me, and on Thy grateful servant look ;
Thy gracious loving-kindness ne'er forsook
 Thy trusting ones ; on Thee alone I cast
My hope and confidence ; Thy holy Book
 Shall be my stay and comfort to the last,
Till in the haven which I seek, my bark made fast

XXXV.

"Shall ride at anchor.   Thou hast blessed my soul
 With bright angelic vision from on high,
And hast vouchsafed before mine eyes t' unroll
 Prophetic outlines of a history
In coming days Thy Name shall magnify :
 Make every soul aglow with holy fire,
That shall to this high enterprise draw nigh,
 And cause them with untiring zeal t' aspire
To win that land for Christ : be this their one desire ! "

XXXVI.

And now my tale has well-nigh reached its goal ;
 My muse hath sung her patriotic lay :
But to what end ?   Perchance some loving soul,
 Allured by tender sympathy, may stay
On life's brief pilgrimage, and while away
 Some weary hour in bending o'er my page,
And, as he readeth, half-unconscious may
 Drink in enthusiasm's noble rage,
And manfully against God's foes resolve to wage

XXXVII.

Undying warfare, spurred by Marsden's zeal ;
   And I shall not have told my tale in vain,
And poesy doth to the heart reveal
   Its hidden secrets, and beguileth pain,
And raiseth minds too prone to entertain
   Idle and foolish reveries ; I bless
My Heavenly Father therefore for the gain
   Versing hath brought me in my loneliness—
'Gainst graceless thoughts defence, and comfort in distress.

XXXVIII.

Seven times this Christian hero to and fro
   From Sydney to New Zealand spread the sail ;
Each time he came, the more his zeal did glow :
   Once was he wrecked ; yet did not courage fail :
Another time saw blood and strife prevail—
   A hand to hand affray—and many fell,*
When suddenly, as in a fairy tale,
   A vessel hove in sight, as it befell—
Rounded the point ; he landed ; all ere long was well :

* "*A pitched battle took place at Kororareka (now called Russell), two miles from Paihia, when the two parties, numbering 600 and 800 respectively, fired at one another at a distance of about twenty yards, and there was a great slaughter. After this, both sides began at heart to wish for peace, but neither knew how to make the first approach, when, two days after the battle, a sail came in sight ; God had sent them a mediator in the person of that devoted friend of their race, Mr. Marsden, whose sixth visit to New Zealand was thus most opportunely timed. The combatants had by this time removed to a distance of several miles from one another, and Mr. Marsden and Mr. H. Williams went from camp to camp on their errand of peace. At length, on the 18th March, 1830, a reconciliation was effected, greatly to the relief of both parties. Again the influence of the missionaries rose high, and Marsden returned once more to New South Wales full of consolation and hope.*"—"*Col. Ch. Histories : New Zealand,*" *pp. 49, 50.*

XXXIX.

From camp to camp Marsden and Williams went,
　　Staying revenge, allaying bitter hate ;
And never, sure, were God's own angels sent
　　On work more Christlike, more compassionate :
Nor was the work of mercy all too late ;
　　Already had their consciences begun
To smite them, and remorse to penetrate
　　Their slow-relenting souls ; the morrow's sun
Saw those peace-makers glad, their glorious victory won.

XL.

To every phase of life there comes a " last "—
　　Last meetings, last addresses, last farewells,
Reviving mournful shadows of things past :
　　Yet glad is it, if each such " last " foretells
The death of death and sorrow ; earth's deathbells
　　Herald the advent of the ever-new,
When " last " shall be no more ; for joyous wells
　　Sprung from Salvation's Rock shall aye renew
The innocent and happy eld with deathless dew.

XLI.

E'en so brave Marsden's visits had their end :
　　He had outlived his span of seventy years ;
But he would die, as he had lived, the friend
　　Of Maori-land ; so heeded not the fears
Of anxious friends, but charmed their listening ears
　　With glowing forecasts of New Zealand's fame ;
Nor rests till once again his course he steers
　　Towards the rising of the Eastern flame,
And lands where Kokianga's fruits shall soon outshame

XLII.

The fabled gardens of the Western Isles :
    Thence to Waimate, in a litter borne
By grateful natives for full forty miles—
    Waimate, whose historic paths were worn
In later years by men whose lives adorn
    By faith's ripe fruits the Church's varied page—
Illustrious Selwyn, Whytehead in life's morn
    Early called home ; by Williams, prelate sage
Of Waiapu, and—relic of that earlier age—

XLIII.

Hadfield, the oft-lamented, oft-restored,
    From Kokianga, as they moved along
The devious path, glad acclamations poured
    On all sides from a swarthy following throng ;
Men, women, children joined in noisy song ;
    Ehoa ! Haere mai ! Tenakoe !
Resounded loud the motley crowd among :
    From all restraint, yet from disorder free—
An unpretending welcome given right heartily.

XLIV.

At Kerikeri, and Paihia's bay
    Warm greetings cheered him 'neath the pastoral roof :
Hence northward to Kaitaia, there to stay
    Till he should bring two bands, who stood aloof
In mutual menace, to give mutual proof
    Of peace desired and amity renewed,
For their own benefit, and in behoof
    Of lonely workers threatened by that feud,
Bearing their lives in hand amid a people rude.

XLV.

Then was exhibited a wondrous scene :
   In the wide, open field a chair was set
Before the Mission House, and soon were seen
   A thousand Natives, from all quarters met,
On the bare ground, content could they but get
   One long last gaze upon that reverend face.
And long they gazed without reproach or let,
   So closely would they each dear feature trace,
That memory's record wasting time might ne'er efface.

XLVI.

Full well they knew they ne'er should see him more ;
   So this last visit to his much loved land
One last long triumph was from shore to shore—
   Not as when captives by the stern command
Of conquering Roman writhed, a sullen band,
   In anguish, to the Consul's chariot bound—
Not such the triumph, but more like that grand
   Meek progress of the Christ on holy ground,
'Midst palm-boughs strewed, and loud Hosannas' joyful
     sound.

XLVII.

Oh ! how they loved him !   And what splendid meed
   Was this for all the travail of his soul !
Enough for toiling, suffering saints to read
   Their guerdon in the skies ; for him the whole
Was not reserved until that final goal :
   And that meek triumph was a preface bright
Of glory which shall spread from pole to pole,
   When Christ shall come to vindicate the right,
And raise on high the champions of faith's lowly fight.

XLVIII.

Methinks I hear the nearer-drawing sound
  Of th' eternal chariot wheels, with murmured song,
Like noise of many waters, circling round ;
  Yet every accent of the myriad throng
Each life's peculiar praises doth prolong,
  Though all attunëd are to harmony :
Ah ! do I hear those white-robed hosts among—
  At least I hail the happy phantasy—
The voice of Marsden chant his own life-melody ?

A LIFE'S AFTERSONG.

I.

Bright, bright the day, and blest the happy hour,
  When first Thy Spirit visited mine heart,
And touched me inwardly with gentle power,
  And bade me straightway on life's mission start.

II.

The Isles were waiting for Thee, gracious Lord ;
  Thy love their mute expressive beauties praised ;
To Thee the fragrance in their forests stored
  The incense of a pure devotion raised.

III.

The coral reefs that circled round their coasts
  By daily growth Thy present might proclaimed,
As round Thy throne the aye-increasing hosts :
  And all dumb nature man's indifference shamed.

IV.

But Thou wast waiting to be gracious; flashed
 Thy sudden light on superstition's gloom ;
The gates of Hell with dismal ruin crashed,
 As when Christ's glory burst the imprisoning tomb.

V.

But lo ! a greater triumph was in store,*
 And Thou didst call me to a higher prize,
When Thou didst ope New Zealand's long-closed door,
 And bid me her dark throngs evangelize.

VI.

How dear those Islands of the eastern main !
 Their sky-aspiring mountains how sublime !
What fadeless forests clothe their fruitful plains !
 How thrills the soul each morn their tuneful chime !

VII.

How bright their sunny skies !   The joyous waves
 That kiss the margin of those myriad bays,
Now softly hymn the love that sinners saves,
 Now, high uplifted, thunder forth the praise

VIII.

Of Him Who reigns in Majesty supreme,
 O'erawes the thoughtless, checks the wanderer's feet.
How dear, New Zealand, each romantic stream,
 That winds among thy hills with murmurings sweet !

---

* *Before setting on foot the New Zealand Mission, Marsden had previously taken an active part in the Mission to the South Sea Islands.*

IX.

Thou blamest not, O Lord, the love that clings
 To such old memories of the former land ;
The beauty, richly poured on earthly things,
 Shall charm a thousandfold whene'er we stand

X.

On Thy new earth, and Thy new heaven admire.
 But chiefly do I bless Thee for the zeal
And love of souls Thy mercy did inspire,
 And that Thou didst my stammering lips unseal

XI.

To preach Thy Gospel to that eager race.
 Blest be Thy Name for every soul that drank
Life from the Fount of Life, and sought Thy face !
 For every rescued soul Thy grace I thank.

XII.

And are the portals of Thy Kingdom closed ?
 Clean gone for ever is redeeming love ?
Can none who have with stubborn heart opposed
 Thy Spirit's pleadings, find a home above ?

XIII.

Deep in the ages lie Thy secrets hid :
 Thou wilt not, oh ! Thou wilt not blame the hope,
Which love's persistent longings still forbid
 To perish utterly, that Thou wilt ope

F

XIV.

A door for the return of outcasts : oh ! it yearns,
   My inmost being yearns, to hear the cry
Of souls repentant, and my spirit burns,
   As in the days of weak mortality,

XV.

To help those dimly struggling into light,
   Oh ! will a day not come when every knee
Shall bow before Thee, humbled by the might
   Of love resistless, every eye shall see

XVI.

Our pierced Redeemer's thorn-encircled brow ;
   And each pierced heart with contrite sorrow own
His grace triumphant ? so the Eternal Now
   Shall see all wills obey His Will alone.

XVII.

Thy Majesty supreme all hearts shall praise,
   O Father ; Thine unceasingly adore,
O holy Saviour ; and to Thine shall raise
   Like worship, Spirit blest, for evermore.

I.

Sonnets of the Old Pilgrim Days of the Canterbury Settlement, New Zealand.

I.

CANTERBURY IN SEPTEMBER, 1853.

(AFTER THE PASSING OF THE CONSTITUTION ACT BY THE BRITISH
PARLIAMENT.)

As when a stream, long chafing to be free
　　From narrowing banks, that do its course refrain,
　　From rocky islet's intercepting chain,
And tangled overgrowth and drifted tree,
Forth bursts at length from dull obscurity,
　　And sweeps majestic through a boundless plain ;
　　So have I seen an infant State remain
Long trammelled by obstructive policy,
Misgovernment, official prejudice ;
　　Numbed by suspense, and chilled by mystery.
　　At length free scope is given.　Behold it rise
Strong, active, self-reliant.　May we see
Who watch thy course with loving, anxious eyes,
　　Thy promise ripen to maturity.

Christchurch, Sep. 23, 1853.

II.

PATRIOTISM.

Ἑλλας ὅπου οἱ Ἕλληνες.
" Greece is where Greeks are."

"'Tis Greece where Greeks do dwell"—so spake and thought
  That ancient race ; the isle-embroidered sea
  Was sprinkled with their towns ; lo ! spreading free
One Greece in many lands.   May we be taught
By them to love our country as we ought !
  'Tis not thy soil, O England ! nor thy scenes
  Though oft on these home-wandering fancy leans ;
'Tis not alone the historic fervour caught
From old association ; not thy marts,
  Nor e'en thy grey cathedrals, nor thy wells
  Of ancient learning, though for these our hearts
May fondly yearn ; true love of country tells
A better tale—thy Church, thy laws, thy arts—
  'Tis England, where an English spirit dwells.

Christchurch, Oct. 3, 1853.

III.

AN HISTORICAL PICTURE.

BEHOLD, O England ! from thy sea-girt throne
  The daughter-nations gathering to thy feet ;
  From east and west, from north and south they meet ;
Those thou hast reared, and claimest for thine own :
Bid them draw near, survey them one by one ;—

See, last of all, before thee trembling stoop
The youngest daughter of the circling group,
By filial look and close resemblance known ;
She kneels before thee, and thy blessing seeks !
  Heir of thy glorious past, she craves to be
  Heir of thy virtues, all that history speaks
Of brave, large-hearted, noble, wise, in thee ;
Thy truth, thy justice, and that light which streaks
  Thy foulest page, thy native piety.

Christchurch, Oct. 10, 1853.

IV.

THE RIVER AVON.

" Fies nobilium tu quoque fontium."—HOR.

I LOVE thee, Avon ! though thy banks have known
  No deed of note ; thy wandering course along
  No Bard of Avon hath poured forth in song
Thy tuneful praise ; thy modest tide hath flown
For ages on, unheeded and alone.
  I love thee for thy English name, but more
  Because my countrymen along thy shore
Have made new homes. Therefore not all unknown
Henceforth thy streams shall flow. A little while
  Shall see thy wastes grow lovely. Not in vain
  Shall England's sons dwell by thee many a mile.
With verdant meads and fields of waving grain
Thy rough uncultured banks ere long shall smile ;
  Heaven-pointing spires shall beautify thy plain.

Christchurch, Oct. 12, 1853.

V.

ON THE ARRIVAL OF THE NEWS OF THE BATTLE OF SINOPE.

"Assyrios complexa sinus stat *opima* Sinope."—VAL. FLAC.

WELL-NIGH two thousand years have sped their flight
   Since the proud Roman trod beneath his feet
   Thy wealth, Sinope ! thy sea-bordering street,
Strewed with barbaric spoil, confessed the might
Of the world's victors.   Still untamed in fight,
   The Pontic hero all undaunted stood,
   A rock unmoved amidst a whelming flood.
Once more Sinope mourns a tearful sight ;
The Northern Eagle swoops, his wrath to wreak
   In savage fury on his helpless prey.
   God help thee, England, to defend the weak !
Who groan beneath Oppression's scorching ray
   Thy island-covert shall not vainly seek ;
   The Tyrant shall not prosper in his day.

Christchurch, May, 1854.

VI.

THE WRECK OF THE SHIP "CANTERBURY ASSOCIATION."

"Non tibi sunt integra lintea . . . .
   Quamvis Pontica pinus,
     Silvæ filia nobilis,
Jactes et genus et nomen inutile . . . .
   Tu, nisi ventis
Debes ludibrium, cave."—AOR. OD. I. 14.

METHOUGHT I saw a gallant goodly bark
   Spread her full canvas to the swelling gale ;
   Honour, right onward steering to her mark,

Sat at the helm, and watched the steady sail ;
Hope at the prow, untired though visions fail,
 Piercing with eagle ken the horizon dark,
 Told of a far-off land her pleasing tale
To listening Faith : Heaven speed thee, gallant bark !
I look again—alas ! another hand
 Guides now the uncertain helm ; a devious way
 'Mid " traps " and " snares " they pass; a pirate band,
Cunning, deception, fraud, usurp the sway :
Hope flees a pilgrim to that far-off land,
 And leaves the bark to howling winds a prey.

Christchurch, August 9, 1854.

NOTE. —*The above Sonnet gives expression to certain vague impressions which were prevalent in Canterbury at the time when it was composed.*

VII.

WAITING FOR THE APPOINTMENT OF A BISHOP.

" Nil sine episcope."—IGNAT.

"Do nought without a Bishop," was the voice
 Of Churchmen in those purer days of old :
 And wonder we why all is poor and cold
Within *our* Zion ?   This one taint alloys
Our fair success.   Our flocks and herds rejoice
 Upon a hundred hills ; our spreading fields
 Stand thick with corn ; God's vineyard only yields
A poor return.   O better, wiser choice
Of ancient days !   When *they* full oft would build
 The Church in distant lands, 'twas thus they thought :
 Seek we a man of God, with wisdom filled,
To be our Master-builder, one who hath fought
Full well the fight of faith, in ruling skilled,
 Gentle and apt to teach, himself God-taught.

Christchurch, Nov. 26, 1854.

II.

Contributions towards a "New Zealand Christian Year." *

I.

A HYMN FOR HOLY THURSDAY.

THOU hast ascended, Lord : may we
In heart and mind ascend with Thee !
With Thee ascend, and with Thee dwell,
To Thee our joys and sorrows tell ;
For Thou to Heaven hast borne with Thee
Thy love and tender sympathy.

It is no vain presumption, Lord,
That bids us soar Thy throne toward ;
Thyself hast said, "Abide in Me ; "
And "Where I am, My own shall be ; "
"Come ye to Me," is ours no less
Than theirs Thou didst on earth address.

'Tis by Thy spirit's promised grace
We sit with Thee in heavenly place,
Where the Great Father, throned in light,
Too dazzling pure for mortal sight,
Yet for Thy sake grants rest above
To spirits purified by love.

* A series of compositions to bear this title, and to emanate from several churchmen
and churchwomen, has more than once been proposed, but has never been carried out.

'Tis of Thy mystic Body said,
We are the members, Thou the Head ;
The members then must yearn to be,
Where dwells the Head in majesty ;
Must heavenward strain their keen desire,
As upward flamed the altar-fire.

What fear we, if to Thee is given
All power and rule in earth and heaven,
And we are Thine ?   If Thou couldst fail,
Then might our watchful foes prevail—
Thy love wax cold, or short Thine arm,
Then cares might drown, and threats alarm.

Blest Stephen saw Thee in his hour,
And bore unmoved the stony shower :
We *see* Thee not, but *know* that Thou
With needful succours strengthenest now
Those who, 'midst suffering's fiercest blaze,
Dare lift to Thee their steadfast gaze.

Then, Lord, increase our faith ; by this
We see Thee on Thy throne, nor miss
The strength Thou sent'st Thy martyred one ;
Thus borne the cross, the fight thus won ;
Thus, dwellers on the earth, may we
In heart and mind ascend with Thee.

Christchurch, May, 1879.

———

II.

HYMN FOR TRINITY SUNDAY.

(COLLECT FOR THE DAY.)

O God the Father, Fount of Love !
O God the Son, that rul'st above !
O God the Spirit, Heavenly Dove !

Taught by Thy word to own Thee Three,
Yet One in glorious Majesty,
We praise, adore, and worship Thee.

As Light and Heat are from the Sun,
Yet Sun and Light and Heat are One,
So own we Father, Spirit, Son.

We cannot scan the mystery,
Nor Thy true Being's secret see,
Yet know Thee on the bended knee ;

Children, we know Thee Father dear ;
Lost ones, we find Thee, Saviour, near ;
Mourners, we own Thee Comforter.

O bliss supreme ; O glad delight !
To lose dim faith, to win clear sight,
To find our darkness turned to light !

To know as we are known, to soar
To higher knowledge evermore,
And deeper depths of love explore !

Pour down meanwhile Thy grace, that we
In this true faith may steadfast be,
And guard us from adversity.

June, 1879.

III.

ST. JAMES: APOSTLE AND MARTYR.

SALOME'S son, ere long to be,
　　Disciple of th' Incarnate Word ;
Unconscious of high destiny,
　　What reck'st thou now of Herod's sword ?

Thine now to gird thy fisher's coat
　　O'er active limbs and supple form,
Deftly to guide the fragile boat,
　　And bravely meet the gathering storm ;

John at thy side ; a loftier choice
　　Awaits you : by that land-girt sea,
Ye soon shall hear a thrilling voice,
　　" Come, leave your nets, and follow Me."

Fishers of men—O glorious toil !
　　If blest the caught, the captors more :
How shall the spoilers o'er such spoil
　　Rejoice on Heaven's eternal shore !

But learn ye first your pride to quell ;
　　Walk by His side ; His meekness see ;
Let love all selfish aims expel,
　　And practise sweet humility.

Invoke ye fire on such as dare
　　His gracious presence to contemn ?
Stay, learn what spirit ye must bear ;
　　He came to save and not condemn.

Ye saw health's flush at His command
  Redden the dead maid's pallid cheek ;
The thousand wonders of His hand
  Ye saw, and Wisdom's self heard speak,

As never man spake.   At His word
  The troubled billows sank to rest ;
His soothing voice, by maniacs heard,
  Hushed the wild trouble of their breast.

With Peter, on that holy height
  Ye saw His glory, and were near,
Ah ! thoughtless sleepers ! on that night,
  To all His fellow-sufferers dear.

Prepare ye now His cup to taste,
  His red baptismal robe to wear ;
Renounce that old ambitious haste
  The patient victor's meed to share.

On thee, O son of thunder ! first,
  For thy bold speech and fiery zeal,
Opposing clouds of fury burst ;
  Thou first didst taste the tyrant's steel ;

Thou first, O James ! of Christ-sent men !
  Now, faithful steward of the Lord's,
With John, and with your comrades ten,
  Reap what He called *your own* rewards :

Not crowns, or robes of glittering show,
  But glories in the soul inwove—
To live the life of God, and grow
  In KNOWLEDGE, HOLINESS and LOVE.

July, 1879.

IV.

ST. BARTHOLOMEW THE APOSTLE.

" BEHOLD, an Israelite indeed,
    And guileless!" thus Messias saith,
As Philip doth Nathanael lead
    To see that man of Nazareth.

" Whence know'st Thou me?" Nathanael cried,
    And, as he spake, his wonder grew:
" Ere Philip called thee," Christ replied,
    " Thee 'neath the fig tree's shade I knew."

" Thou art the Son of God!" exclaimed
    The Saint—such sudden faith did spring,
Soon as he heard the fig tree named—
    " O Rabbi, Thou art Israel's King!"

What stirred so deep Nathanael's heart?
    That spark electric lit the whole
Of memory's train with lightning dart,
    And flashed conviction to his soul.

For who but One can pierce the breast?
    The secret of that lonely hour
Who knew, could fathom all the rest;
    And whose but God's that wondrous power?

O childlike faith! O candour rare!
    Not spurning reason for its guide,
But sifting all with jealous care,
    Yet prompt to follow light supplied!

Such faith shall grow from strength to strength,
    And "greater things" shall aye descry,
Till to the sin-purged soul at length
    Heaven's glories all shall open lie.

Such men are God's own princes true,
    With Him shall wrestle and prevail;
To such pure souls He will renew
    Their exiled Father's wondrous tale—

The stairway set 'twixt earth and heaven
    With angels bearing prayers aloft,
And angels bringing blessings given—
    Gifts wrapt in sombre covering oft.

But He from Whom such commerce springs—
    Ascending prayer, descending grace—
Is He Who into union brings
    The Godhead with our human race.

He is the Stair; through Him ascends
    Each prayer we breathe to Heavenly Love:
Through Him alone each boon descends
    On angel-pinions from above.

Come then to Him, all ye who doubt;
    O come, and with Nathanael's faith
And candour search this question out—
    HATH GOOD COME OUT OF NAZARETH?

August, 1879.

V.

FEAST OF ST. MICHAEL AND ALL ANGELS.

HOLY Angels, robed in glory,
    Fain would we your praises sing,
Fain resound in grateful story,
    So that heaven and earth should ring,
All your ministries of love,
Shed on man from God above.

Like the dew in autumn morning,
    Viewless, noiseless, gliding down—
Like the sheen of light adorning
    Some old mountain's joy-lit crown—
Blessing thus, ye come and go,
But your pathway who can know?

What though, like the rushing torrent,
    Ye make havoc and destroy,
Executing God's high warrant,
    Dashing down men's cup of joy;
Hastening to perform His will,
Smite or rescue, save or kill:

What thou, wrapped in garb mysterious,
    Seem ye ministers of doom,
Veiling love 'neath aspect serious,
    Hiding mercy under gloom—
Mystery shall end with night,
Gloom be turned to endless light.

Flamed *one* sword at Eden's portal,
　Angel-borne, to guard the way :
When the Prince of Life immortal,
　Fought for us and won the day
And did Paradise regain,
Hosts of Angels thronged His train.

" Praise to God in highest Heaven !
　Peace ! goodwill ! the Christ is born ! "
With such sounds the sky was riven
　On that first glad Christmas morn :
Friends of man, our joy ye share !
Gladly our new birth declare !

When before the Man of Sorrow,
　Satan, lord of darkness, quailed,
On that night's triumphant morrow
　Your due ministries availed
To refresh the Lord of Life,
Wearied with that sinless strife.

When His human spirit languished,
　Bowed 'neath crushing loads of grief,
To His soul so keenly anguished
　One bright seraph brought relief—
Wonder vast surpassing thought !
To his *Lord* and *Maker* brought !

Death before Him fled defeated—
　Watched ye round the open tomb :
Now He reigns in glory seated,
　Till shall break that Dawn of Doom :
When He comes to earth again,
Ye shall form His countless train.

Shed meanwhile on heirs of glory
   Comfort in the midst of woes ;
Intersperse their life's dull story
   With bright days and calm repose :
O'er the penitent rejoice,
Help us lift the suppliant voice —

Help us praise the only Giver,
   Lord of men and angels too :
Help us when we cross the river
   That divideth us from you :
When the mortal body dies,
Bear our souls to Paradise.

Dimly now we scan the traces
   Of your ministering hands :
When shall we behold the faces
   Of your pure, bright, loving bands ?
Through the dark one glimpse to gain
   Yearn our hearts, but all in vain.

Oh ! what joy when we shall mingle
   In your sweet societies,
And, while loving all, shall single
   From your myriad companies—
Principalities and Powers—
Each his *Guardian* of past hours.

Now from earthly station lowly
   Join we your full choirs on high,
Singing HOLY, HOLY, HOLY !
   To the adored Trinity,
In one glorious anthem blending,
Aye beginning, never ending.

September, 1879.

G

VI.

ST. LUKE THE EVANGELIST.
(October 18.)

THIRD of the blessed Four,
   From thee is named this Day :
O Holy Ghost ! be pleased to pour
   On us some kindling ray,
That, as from holy Luke we learn
The Gospel lore, our hearts may burn
   Within us on life's way.

How sweetly on the mind,
   Those gracious accents fall,
When he, whom Roman fetters bind,
   God's chosen warrior, Paul,
Doth Luke, his fellow-soldier tried,
In peril clinging to his side,
   " Beloved Physician " call.

O ! may the healing Voice,
   That speaks from out his page,
Make every broken heart rejoice,
   And sound from age to age,
To cure the plague of every heart,
To bind the wounds from every dart,
   Hurled by fell Satan's rage !

Those sweetest Gospel-hymns
   Echo all time along ;
No lapse of years their freshness dims—
   The Blessed Virgin's Song —
And Benedictus, glorious word !
Old Simeon's Nunc Dimittis heard
   The Temple courts among—

The angelic burst of praise
  By shepherds heard at night—
And shall not ransomed sinners raise
  Like songs for gifts of light ?
Let glad Magnificats arise ;
Your Benedictus to the skies
  Uplift with all your might.

Thou lov'st, O Luke, to write
  How oft the Lord did pray ;
How oft with blessing sons of light
  Came down, thou lov'st to say :
May we the prayer of faith be taught,
And for each boon by angels brought
  Our thankful tribute pay !

The comforts thou hast stored
  Sin's mourners aye shall reach ;
The Pardoned One at Simon's board
  Poor outcasts hope shall teach :
The Prodigal's sweet soothing tale,
The Publican's accepted wail,
  Peace to the contrite preach.

Thy pictured scenes how meet
  To touch the thoughtful heart !
See Mary sit at Jesus' feet,
  Choosing the better part !
See Lazarus and Dives stand
As beacons clear on either hand
  A bridgeless gulf apart !

What mangled form is this?
   Who these that coldly turn?
Those mute appealing wounds, I wis,
   Might make the coldest burn:
Cometh a lowlier Stranger by;
Samaria's garb and mien I spy;
   Such woe *He* will not spurn.

Two friends in converse high,
   Yet sad, and doubt-oppressed,
Behold a Stranger drawing nigh,
   Who strangely them addressed—
Ah! now their hearts within them burn,
As from His lips they awe-struck learn
   Truths their own souls confessed.

" Abide with us," they prayed,
   " Fast fall the shades of night :"
So to their social meal He stayed,
   And filled their souls with light :
He took the Bread—their wonder grew—
The Bread He brake—ah! now they knew—
   But He was lost to sight.

Thy Light within us pour,
   That in the Broken Bread
Our hearts may know Thee and adore,
   And with Thyself be fed !
And guide us to the Perfect Light,
Where Thou wilt ne'er be lost to sight,
   Our Saviour and our Head !

October, 1879.

VII.

ALL SAINTS' DAY.

" Who are these like stars appearing?"—HYMNS A. & M., 427.

IN many ways the Saints are like the stars,
This first—they are so pure ; no shadow mars,
In stars or saints, their perfect loveliness.
Sin-spotted, true ! was once the earthly dress
Of God's elect, but they have washed it white
In the Lamb's Blood, and now 'tis starry-bright.
   Sweet, gentle, modest is the light that beams
From starry spheres ; its tender radiance seems
To shed soft dewy blessings where it falls ;
Not like the sudden comet, which appals,
And frights a sinful world with boding glare :
So Christ's true saints make not their light to flare
For self-elation, but so let it shine
That all may glorify the Source Divine,
Who soweth a dark world with beams of light,
And setteth saints, like stars, to gild our night.
   There is no jealousy 'twixt star and star,
'Twixt saint and fellow-saint ; though brighter far
One than another, each one only tries
To shine his brightest in his Maker's eyes.
Some softly gleam, breathing delicious sense
Of trustful hope serene ; with glow intense,
Emblems of fervent hope and burning zeal,
Others seem all on fire ; beholders feel
Themselves with holy passion all aglow :
Perpetual founts of sparkling radiance flow
From others, cheering gloom, though oft opprest
Themselves by secret troubles of the breast :

As gems in order set, of varied hue,
Form one bright crown, all beautiful to view,
For His dear glory each his lustre gives,
From Whom, for Whom, in Whom alone he lives.
   Mark this again ; the stars are hid from sight,
While gaudy day displays his garish light ;
Yet are they there to comfort and to cheer,
When darksome night lets fall her curtain drear :
Who sees not here an image true, though faint,
Of that which haps with many an earthly saint ?
While life flows on all prosperous and gay,
We pass them undistinguished on our way,
Discerning nought of brightness ; but let pain,
Or other of the melancholy train
Of life's calamities o'ercloud our scene,
And straightway God's own light-bearers are seen
Out-shining sudden on our night of grief ;
Our full hearts seek, and find the sought relief :
That they are Christ's, by this sure sign we know—
Their Christ-like sympathy for others' woe.
   List to one more resemblance ; see afar
That exquisitely pure and lovely star :
It shines on fields of carnage, yet is pure ;
On sooty furnaces—its beams endure
In undiminished loveliness—on heaps
Of loathsome garbage, yet its brightness keeps
Undimmed, unsullied.   So the pure in heart
Walk in the midst of sin, yet live apart :
Souls wrapped in their own atmosphere of grace
No foul contagious vapours can debase :
Though forced to dwell 'mid throng of unclean lips,
Their heavenly brightness suffers no eclipse :

'Mid dens of squalid infamy and dirt
The saintly Sister moves and takes no hurt :
Not all unlike our Master Christ, Who came,
And dwelt in likeness of our sinful frame
For thrice eleven years, and with man's eyes
Saw all man's deeds of guilt, and heard his lies,
His passionate ravings, his foul words of shame,
And knew more evil than the tongue can name,
Yet knew it all *without*, and not *within :*
The leaguered hosts of darkness could not win
One instant's lodgment in that holy shrine,
Where dwelt and tabernacled Light Divine.

   May we be numbered with Thy saints, O Lord !
And bright examples, like the stars, afford
Of pureness, constant service, purpose high
Wrought out with lowliness and modesty,
In place or high or low, as God shall choose !
O may we strive ourselves in Thee to lose,
Nor grudge another's praise, but mark with joy
Some gifted mind its higher light employ
In worthier service than our powers can give !
May we illume our neighbour's night, and live
'Mid foul contagion round us, still the same,
Unsullied by the breath of guilt and shame !

November, 1879.

VIII.

ADVENT.

WHAT strange mysterious feelings throng our souls,
　　As on Thine advent, gracious Lord, we dwell !
Joy blends with wonder ; yet strong awe controls
　　All less emotions by its potent spell.

Lord ! can it be that we shall hear and live,
　　The Archangel's summons, and the trump of God ?
Hear Thine own Voice the startling order give,
　　Shall open every grave the world abroad ?

And wilt Thou rend the heavens and come down ?
　　And shall we see in long procession wind
The apocalyptic vision which shall crown
　　The age-long expectation of mankind ?

All Heaven shall come to earth, and earth shall see
　　Once more her Maker on her bosom stand :
Once more, no longer in humility,
　　His feet shall tread that glorious Holy Land.

Mount Olivet His parting footsteps pressed ;
　　Mount Olivet shall welcome His return—
Mount Olivet, above all mountains blessed,
　　Shall welcome Him for Whom all nations yearn.*

And shall we see Thy face ?　That vision sweet,
　　Yet awful, sure, will thrill us through and through ;
But that Thy love shall stay our trembling feet,
　　Our weakness must that dread amazement rue :

---

* *S.e St. Luke xcic. 50, 51 ; Acts i. 1! ; Zech. xiv. 4.*

But Thou wilt strengthen us, as when of old
   Thy frail one's fears Thou gently didst upbraid ;
The same inspiring Voice shall make *us* bold :
   " Be of good cheer ; 'tis I ; be not afraid."

Then shall we know Thee Whom we have believed—
   Yes, know Thee, Lord, as we by Thee are known ;
Thy promise never hath man's trust deceived ;
   Thy faithful servants' work Thou then wilt own.

Then shall Thy sweetness, Lord, shed richer joy,
   Than Heaven itself with treasured glories rife ;
Then shall we find—O bliss without alloy !
   Thy loving-kindness better than the life.

Yet shalt Thou judge the world in majesty
   And seraphs shall their radiant faces veil ;
The Judgment set, the books shall opened be,
   And all the kindreds of the earth shall wail.

All unrepented sin shall then lie bare ;
   From Thy soul-piercing sight no fraud shall lurk ;
Thy Book's unfailing record shall declare
   Each idle word and each unholy work.

Who may abide that Judgment ?   Lord, we plead
   The boundless merit of Thy Sacrifice ;
Thy Blood hath cleansed the guilt of thought and deed ;
   Thy love shall make us stainless in Thine eyes.

Yet fill us, gracious Lord, with holy fear ;
   Graft in our hearts unfeigned humility ;
And help us, be the cost however dear,
   To tread in all Thy footsteps carefully.

And thus prepare us for that solemn Day ;
  So shall we stand upright before Thy Throne,
Upheld by Thee—then, Lord, no more delay,
  But come, come quickly to redeem Thine own !

December, 1879.

IX.

WHO RUNS MAY READ.

A FRIEND had stayed with me for many days,
And grown into my life, when suddenly
He said, " My time is come, and I must go "—
And so departed without other word :
  Straightway there entered at another door
An airy, dainty creature, nimble-footed,
With onward-peering eyes and wondering gaze,
And features—no, not features—outlines vague,
Mere possibilities—in sooth he seemed
Not so much being as about to be.
Arrayed he was in vesture smooth and white,
Like softest vellum, trailing after him
In train of many folds, all ruled with lines
As though for writing on, but nothing writ.
  I could not but accost him : " Child," I cried,
"Say who thou art, and whence, and what thy name?"
He thus replied in tones of startling depth,
Deep as a murmur from an ocean cave :
" Adown the slanting moonbeam's silver stair,
Born in the noon of summer night, I come,
The youngest child of Hope and Father Time ;
A stroke, two figures serpentine, and then

A cypher spell a name by me first borne :
Though newly-born, I bear within my breast
The lessons of well-nigh six thousand years,
And therefore claim I right to counsel thee ;
And, first, I bring thee this "—with that I saw
Beneath his robe a curious packet sealed
With numerous seals—"Each opening morn," he said,
" One of these seals will open, and disclose
Thy lot and portion for each several day :
Desire no more to know ; seek not to break
One seal before its date ; but do and bear
The duty and the burden of the hour
With constancy and fearless trust in God.
Let duty be thy care, not happiness :
Thy God, if thou but seek to do His will,
And with thine heart do love and serve His Son,
With bounteous hand will all thy need supply.
He that seeks happiness, pursues a dream,
And wakes to disappointment ; he who lives
For truth and duty, and unswerving treads
The one right path in trouble and in joy,
Looking to Christ, shall find true happiness—
Shall find in God, the Holy Three-in-One,
A Father and a Brother and a Friend."
   " And wilt thou go ? " I said, and he replied,
" Nay, I will stay with thee for many days,
And walk with thee, and grow into thy life,
As he that just departed ; but though now
My form seem strange, I shall familiar grow,
And soon shall walk unnoticed by thy side,
Till I wax old, and all at once depart ;
But if thou use me well, a Day shall come,

When I will speak for thee before the Throne :
But now, I pray thee, treasure up my words ;
Be brave and patient, just and temperate ;
Be tender and forgiving, full of love
To God and man, and so God prosper thee ! "
    And thus he ended : may his thrilling words
Pour through my senses, filter through my heart,
And issue day by day, by God's sweet grace,
In the pure fountain of a blameless life !

January 1st, 1880.

X.

THE PRESENTATION OF CHRIST IN THE TEMPLE,

COMMONLY CALLED THE PURIFICATION OF ST. MARY THE VIRGIN.

LORD ! humbly at Thy feet
    Our offerings now we lay,
And tune our choicest hymns to greet
    Thy Presentation Day.

Within the Temple gates
    The Holy Maid doth bear
Thine infant form, while Joseph waits,
    And makes her wants his care.

To Thine own Temple, Lord,
    Thou camest all unknown :
The Son, by angel-hosts adored,
    No priest on earth doth own.

Yet were there faithful hearts
　To whom Thou wast revealed :
To childlike souls God aye imparts
　Light from the proud concealed.

Such was the aged seer,
　Who clasped Thee to his breast,
And thus, in words to Christians dear,
　His thankful joy expressed :

" Now lettest Thou, O Lord,
　Thy servant go in peace,
And dost his waiting soul afford
　A glad, a kind release :

" For now mine eyes behold
　Salvation long designed,
The glory of Thy flock of old,
　A Light for all mankind ! "

Nor Asher's daughter less
　Her faithful witness bore,
The Temple-haunting prophetess,
　The widow of fourscore.

The joy within her born,
　She straightway shared with them
Who looked for glad redemption's morn
　In old Jerusalem.

Like precious faith we crave ;
　May we like witness bear,
And love in every gift we have
　To see our brethren share !

And thus Thy servants pray
   Each year with fervour fresh—
As Thou presented wast this day
   In substance of our flesh,

So we before Thy throne
   May be presented pure,
And share for ever with Thine own,
   True joys that aye endure.

February, 1880.

XI.

THE ANNUNCIATION OF THE BLESSED VIRGIN MARY.

WHAT tale so dear to holy thought,
   What theme to sacred Muse so sweet,
As that glad news by Gabriel brought
   This day the Virgin's ear to greet?

Glad news, but passing strange, I ween:
   The wondrous truths her faith received
No ear had heard, no eye had seen,
   Nor had the heart of man conceived.

O glorious truths! transcendent grace!
   O source of wonder ever fresh!
A Virgin's Son should save the race,
   And God should dwell in human flesh!

What rushing tides of mingled thought
   Surged through the Virgin's heart amain!
O tidings strange! What had God wrought?
   O awful joy! O care-fraught gain!

Yet meekly bowed that lowly Maid,
  And bent her will submissively
To bear the burden on her laid,
  And bide the opening mystery.

These memorable words she spake,
  " Behold the handmaid of the Lord ! "
God gave, and she would simply take—
  " Be it according to Thy word ! "

O shall we not her name revere ?
  O shall we not her memory bless ?
Oft as the angelic " Hail " we hear,
  Oft as our lips our Creed confess ?

Oft as we chant at Evensong,
  From day to day, from week to week,
How God, through all the ages long,
  Confounds the proud, exalts the meek ?

Thrice blest in this, that she received
  High privilege's matchless crown ;
But rather blest, that she *believed*,
  And 'neath the will of God bowed down !

Fain would we ponder, Virgin blest !
  With faith like thine Truth's mystery :
He honours best, who follows best
  Thy lowliness, thy purity.

March, 1880.

XII.

EASTER-TIDE IN AUTUMN.

OLD England's sacred poets often sing
How aptly Easter-tide falls in with Spring ;
How Nature's resurrection seems to preach
In parable what Holy Writ doth teach—
The bud that cleaves the bark, the vigorous shoot,
That springeth upward from the buried root ;
The haggard boughs that don their leafy screen ;
The dull, dead landscape, flushing into green ;
The insect-peopled air, the wakened hive,
The dew-bespangled pastures all alive
With the blithe younglings of the flock and herd,
And hedgerows musical with song of bird :—
Nature's full choir thus sings of hope and trust,
Life from the dead, renewal from the dust.

But what of us in this far Southern clime,
Whose Easter falls in Autumn's mellow time,
When each decaying leaf, and fading flower,
Suggests that we are creatures of an hour ?
Where is hope's stay ? and where our stable ground
Of comfort, with all nature dying round?
We answer thus, " We boldly take our stand,
Not on weak, changeful Nature's shifting sand,
But on firm Revelation's changeless Rock,
Founded whereon our faith sustains the shock,
Unmoved, of dying Nature's omens drear :
Faith is hope's stay, the antidote of fear :
In Christ Who died, yea rather Who is risen,
We trust to raise us from the grave's dark prison.
Though nature dies, " Fear not," the Spirit saith,
" 'Tis faith helps nature, and not nature faith."

Easter, 1880.

XIII.

A HYMN TO THE HOLY SPIRIT.

As breathes o'er countless fields sweet balmy Spring
  And wakes the hidden life in every spray,
And tunes each woodland warbler's throat to sing,
  So breathe new life into our souls, we pray,
     Thou gracious Spirit blest !

As falls refreshing dew on pastures dry,
  And every meadow flushes into green,
So shed on us Thy bounteous grace, we cry,
  Reviving all our soul's world-jaded scene,
     Thou gracious Spirit blest !

As beams right welcome on the midnight sky
  The anxious mariner's long-watched-for star,
So guide right onward to our home on high,
  Lest in the dark we grope and wander far,
     Thou gracious Spirit blest !

As all that weary desert journey through
  The Fiery Cloud o'ershadowed Israel's camp,
So by Thy presence and indwelling true
  Be our unfailing Stay, our Strength, our Lamp,
     Thou gracious Spirit blest !

Thee, sweet refreshing Spring, and Fount of grace,
  Thee, guiding, gladdening Star, we aye adore,
Thee, Strength and Comforter throughout our race,
  With Father, and with Son, for evermore,
     Thou gracious Spirit blest !

Whitsun Eve, 1891.

*The above Hymn was thought out in the watches of the night on board the N. Z.
Shipping Company's R. M. S. " Kaikoura," in the South Pacific Ocean, in the course
of the return voyage from England to New Zealand.*

H

XIV.

HYMN FOR THE CONSECRATION OF A BISHOP.

LORD, our prayer to Thee addressing,
  Kneel we at Thy throne to-day ;
May Thy Spirit's fullest blessing
  Guide and guard Thy servant's way,
Whom with solemn rite our fathers
  Bless and consecrate to-day.

May there shine in all his teaching
  Living light from out Thy word,
That true wisdom through his preaching
  On Thy flock may be outpoured,
And a good account be rendered
  At the advent of the Lord.

May he faithfully admonish
  Erring souls, sustain the weak,
Urge the slow, the guilty punish,
  Cheer the humble, raise the meek,
Shield the poor, and, like his Master,
  To reclaim the outcast seek.

Led by him, Lord, may we enter
  Paths of self-devotion high,
While our trust on Thee we centre,
  Live to Thee, and to Thee die ;
Lord, for Thee and for our neighbour,
  Spent and spending joyfully.

May he ever follow duly
   Steps of apostolic men,
Lead a saintly life and truly
   Well-earned praise shall greet him then,
" Shews he forth, as true successor,
   Lives pourtrayed by sacred pen."

In deep grief or sharp affliction,
   Hours of toil or timely rest,
May Thy gracious benediction
   Hope impart and patience blest ;
And hereafter to Thy servant
   All Thy glory manifest.

The above Hymn was set to music by F. G. Tendall, Esq., Mus. Bac., Oxon, Organist of the Cathedral, and sung at the consecration of the Right Rev. Churchill Julius, D.D. to the Bishopric of Christchurch, New Zealand, on the Feast of SS. Philip and James, 1890.

XV.

A SONG OF THE CHURCH.

" Her foundations are upon the holy hills."

WE love our Church, the English Church,
   The Church of the olden time,
Yet ever new with the glistening dew,
   That freshened her early prime.

She holds the faith, the once-taught faith—
   Her witness knows no change—
Yet margin finds for differing minds
   Within her ample range.

She guards the Word, the sacred Word,
   Inspired by God's own breath,
And spreads its light to the sons of night,
   That sit 'neath shades of death.

She holds two holy Sacraments,
   Pledges of love divine :
New Birth God-given—true Bread from Heaven—
   Each has its own fit sign.

The apostolic line she claims,
   Yet rather loves to prove
Her high descent by the argument
   Of works that spring from love.

We cherish her old ritual,
   So simple yet so grand :
Her stirring chant makes true hearts pant
   For the life of the better land.

Her sweet responsive Litany
   Brings heaven before our eyes :
Her altar-rite—our chief delight —
   Dearly as life we prize.

We bear her name the wide world o'er,
   And wheresoe'er we roam,
We wear the trace of our Mother's face,
   And boast of our island-home.

Return, ye long-lost ones, return !
   Your Mother opens wide
Her loving breast to give you rest,
   Nor will your wandering chide.

O why should discord waste our strength?
    Let all who have one hope
United stand, to front the band,
    That dares with Christ to cope.

Join hearts to love the grand old Church,
    And in her tuneful quires
Be Christ the Lord by all adored,
    With song that never tires.

XVI.

TO SUNDAY SCHOOL TEACHERS.

" Feed My lambs."—St. John xxi. 15.

" Whoso shall receive one such little child in My Name receiveth Me."
St. Matt. xviii. 5.

BETHINK thee, Christian teacher,
    Whose work thou hast in hand,
As those few simple children
    Before thee take their stand.

If Holy Church hath set thee
    To teach within her school ;
If that young flock thou teachest
    'Neath thine own pastor's rule ;

Then may'st thou know thy Saviour
    Is calling unto thee,
From His high throne in heaven,
    "Go, feed those lambs for Me."

Grave in thine heart His saying,
    Nor let its trace grow dim,
" Who in His Name receiveth
    One child, receiveth Him."

Bethink thee then how precious
    The lowliest in that group
To Him, Who to redeem us
    From heaven to earth did stoop.

O think what condescension
    The King of kings hath shown—
To quit His ancient glory,
    To leave His Father's throne ;

To make His home with sinners
    For thirty years and more ;
To be the scorned of scorners,
    To dwell among the poor.

Then deem we all too little
    Our utmost service paid,
To quit in poorest measure
    The sacrifice He made.

When wise and great men bend them
    Some lowly class to teach,
His lowliness they copy,
    But know they cannot reach.

Scan well those homely features—
    Thou canst not *see* thy Lord :
But was it ever told thee
    That *sight* should win reward ?

Believe, and do not question ;
   By faith thy Master see :
" Whoso one child receiveth,"
   He said, " receiveth Me."

Go, *act* on that assurance,
   And, if thou persevere,
" Well done, thou faithful servant,"
   Ere long thy soul shall hear.

July, 1880.

XVII.

THE TRANSFIGURATION.

" And He was transfigured before them."—St. MARK IX. 2.

GLORIOUS vision, that didst lighten
   Erst the Saviour's path of woe,
And with lingering beam dost brighten
   Our sin-darkened walk below,
Shining on my world-worn heart,
Brief poetic glow impart !

See in stately isolation
   Tabor's solemn Mount uprise,
Fitting scene for contemplation,
   Holy commerce with the skies :
Thither see the Lord ascend ;
See the faithful Three attend.

Now, the summit gained, behold Him
    Bending low in solemn prayer :
Seraph wings unseen enfold Him,
    As He kneeleth humbly there :
Hush ! ye winds ! and every sound
Cease in earth and air around !

As He prayeth, streams of brightness,
    Lightning-like, upon Him pour ;
Sudden sheen of dazzling whiteness
    Silvers all His raiment o'er :
Shineth as the sun His face,
Radiant with surpassing grace.

Stood that instant by Messias
    Glorious forms from out the sky—
Stood both Moses and Elias,
    As they lived in days gone by :
With this scene what else can vie
In our world's long history ?

Yet their talk was not of glory ;
    Spake they of the Lord's decease,
Calvary's sweet awful story,
    And the Cross, whence comes our peace :
Solemn converse, long and deep,
While the Three are wrapped in sleep !

Slept the Three, but on their waking
    Peter spake in sudden scare
Hasty words about the making
    Of three tabernacles there—
As though Christ were e'en as they—
For he wist not what to say.

Quickly a bright cloud o'erspread them,
   Like that Cloud that erst did bless
With its light God's host, and led them
   Through the dreadful wilderness :
From the Cloud, O wondrous love !
Spake the Voice of God above—

Voice, that at the world's creating,
   Spake the word, and it was done—
Said, in tones soul-penetrating
   " This is My beloved Son ; "
And, as those two forms grew dim,
Thus continued, " Hear ye Him."

As the light of planets waneth
   In thy light, O glorious Sun !
None before the face remaineth
   Of God's sole-begotten One,
Who doth by a word create
Prophets, Kings, earth's greatest great.

May Thy love, our hearts bedewing,
   Fill us full of light divine !
May Thy grace, our souls renewing,
   Make us as Thy saints to shine !
And that we that grace may share,
Make us to be much in prayer !

September, 1880.

III.

Fragments of an unfinished Cantata entitled "Pentecost."

---

1. ON THE WAY TO THE MOUNT OF OLIVES.

(Acts i. 4, 5.)

The Apostles.　DEAREST Master, must Thou leave us
　　　　　　　· Orphaned, desolate, forlorn ?
　　　　　　　Sore Thou know'st Thy loss will grieve us :
　　　　　　　Wanting Thee, can life be borne ?

The Lord.　　Rest ye trustful and obedient ;
　　　　　　　Let not fears distress your heart :
　　　　　　　Said I not, " It is expedient
　　　　　　　I should from your sight depart ;
　　　　　　　So the Holy Spirit blest
　　　　　　　Shall be with you, shall be near you,
　　　　　　　Ever dwell within your breast ;
　　　　　　　Guide you, quicken you, and cheer you,
　　　　　　　Give you strength, and peace, and rest.

The Apostles. Yet will rage both Jew and Roman,
  Furiously rage together;
We shall quail before the foeman,
  Like frail barks in stormy weather.

The Lord. Ah ! faithless ones, be strong, be strong;
  Full well I know the flesh is weak;
But list ! ye shall not tarry long;
  For soon shall come, His flock to seek
The Holy Ghost ! baptismal fire
  Ere many days shall on you light,
And your weak, timid souls inspire
  With heav'n-sent strength, and new-born
    might;
No quailing then, but keen desire
  Men's souls to save, for God to fight.

2. THE WEEK OF EXPECTATION.

A HYMN OF SYMPATHY.

(To be sung by the Congregation.)

"Twas thus He bade them calmly wait,
  Nor be dismayed, whate'er betide;
Then in their sight ascending, sate
  Majestic by His Father's side.

Captivity He captive led,
  And gifts received for rebel man—
One crowning Gift, which He had said
  Should arm them, ere their work began.

And so they wait in wonder calm,
  Though every day a century seem,
And soothe their hearts with text and psalm,
  Though yearning for hope's dawning beam.

Full well they know the promise sure,
    Nor will its coming tarry long;
Full well they know it will endure,
    And make them brave and wise and strong.

But what the form, and what the sign,
    In silent awe they contemplate;
To know in full the truth divine,
    Needs must they in obedience wait.

So, when our latter end draws nigh,
    May faith be clear, and patience strong,
Our hearts with thrilling hope beat high,
    Although the Day-star tarry long.

Ear hath not heard, eye hath not seen,
    Nor can the heart of man conceive,
The glorious things our God doth mean
    For all who in His Christ believe.

Hope on, hope ever; hope deferred
    May sicken many a fainting soul;
But when He comes—have we not heard?—
    The Bread of Life shall make us whole.

3. PRAYER OF THE ASSEMBLED APOSTLES ON THE DAY
                    OF PENTECOST.

The holy Day is come;
    Lord, in Thy Name we meet;
O send Thy promised mercy down
    From Thy celestial seat.

Lord, clothe us now with might,
 And wisdom past all thought :
Be this, e'en this the accepted hour,
 And work as Thou hast wrought :

As when the Red Sea clove
 Before Thy ransomed flock,
And Pharaoh's realm with terror reeled,
 And Satan's felt the shock.

Or as, when Sinai's height
 With flame was all ablaze,
The awe-struck tribes the Law received
 In terror and amaze.

Pour down Thy gracious rain ;
 Baptize us with Thy fire ;
Make glad Thine own inheritance ;
 Fulfil their heart's desire.

So will we preach Thy word
 To earth's remotest shore ;
And spread Thy Kingdom far and wide,
 Till time shall be no more.

4.   THE AMAZEMENT AND DOUBT OF THE MULTITUDE
    AT THE MIRACLE OF TONGUES.

The Seriously   Are not these all Galileans ?
 Impressed.   How then do we hear them speak,
    Every man in his own language,
     I a Roman, you a Greek—

Yonder man from far Cyrene,
　　This Pamphylian, that Arabian,
　　This from Pontus, that from Crete—
　Sure signs you trace
　In each man's face,
That what these eager speakers mean, he
　　Comprehends; you see them greet
　　　With earnest eyes,
　　　And glad surprise,
The wondrous things of which they treat.

The Scoffers.　Fools ye are! these Galileans
　　By their speech themselves bewray:
　　Drunk with wine—this, this the secret:
　　Why give heed to what they say?

The Seriously　Ah! no; it must be something higher:
　Impressed.　　See ye not upon their faces
　　Radiant glow of light divine?
　　　Each eye is fired;
　　　Each tongue inspired;
　　Such words, such looks come not from wine.
　　God hath sent these men to tell
　　　Some gracious news,
　　　And joy diffuse
　　'Mong people that in darkness dwell.

5. ST. PETER ADDRESSES THE MULTITUDE.

My brother-men, give heed to me, and ponder what I say:
Think not these men are drunk with wine, thus early in the
　　day.

A great outpouring of His grace the Lord our God hath
    willed,

And Joel's ancient prophecy is in your ears fulfilled :

"The latter days shall teem," saith God, "with signs and
    wonders fresh,

And I will pour abundantly My Spirit on all flesh :

Your young men shall see visions, and your old men shall
    dream dreams ;

The sun shall turn to darkness, and the moon shall hide
    her beams."

These things are but beginnings of a wondrous age to rise,

When that great Day and notable shall dawn before your
    eyes :

Now opens wide the Kingdom ; all shall enter in who strive ;

For whoso calleth on the Lord, shall save his soul alive.

    Now hearken, men of Israel : Jesus of Nazareth,

Whom Pilate innocent adjudged, but ye condemned to death,

And though approved by miracle among you and by sign,

And by a thousand mighty works declared to be Divine,

Yet ye by wicked hands have seized and crucified and slain—

Him God hath loosed from pains of death, and raised to
    life again ;

For did not Royal David in the Book of Psalms affirm,

"Thou shalt not leave My soul in hell, nor shall this flesh
    the worm

Consume?" Now David—may I boldly speak?—long
    since was laid

Unto his fathers ; but these words he by the Spirit said

Concerning Christ, that He should not in bonds of death
    remain,

But that our God those bonds should loose, and raise Him
    up again :

Moreover He hath lifted Him to His right hand on high,
Where now He sits in glory on His throne above the sky :
And lo ! to make His promise good, and bring His King-
 dom near,
Hath shed abroad His Holy Ghost—whence this ye see
 and hear.
Let all the house of Israel then hold fast this faithful word,
" Jesus the Crucified is made for aye both Christ and Lord."

6. St. Peter's Second Address, *when the people were
"pricked in their heart and said . . . . Men and
brethren, what shall we do ?"*

 Repent, and turn to God with all your soul,
  And be baptized each one in Jesus' Name :
 Faith in His saving Name shall make you whole,
  And He shall wash you clean from guilt and shame.

 The fount of life now opened freely runs ;
  The Lord will of His Spirit richly give :
 The Promise is to you and to your sons ;
  O come ye to the waters ; drink and live.

 Nor, brothers, is our word for you alone ;
  A universal Message sent to all
 'Tis ours to preach ; but, first, to you His own,
  And then to those the Lord our God shall call.

 Salvation, oh ! salvation we proclaim ;
  The Lord invites the humble and the meek ;
 A covert and a refuge 'neath His Name
  From this untoward generation seek.

7. HYMN OF THE BAPTIZED.

(To be sung by the Congregation.)

Free and bounteous are Thy mercies, God of hosts, Almighty
  Lord,
Who hast called us to Thy Kingdom, and redeemed us by
  Thy word:
Loudly we exalt Thy praises, joyfully extol Thy Name;
All the listening world rejoicing of Thy works shall hear the
  fame.

Men of old with pride disdainful, threatening to besiege the
  sky,
Built a tower to heaven upreaching, to defy Thy Majesty:
Thou didst scatter and confound them, and didst bring
  their plans to nought,
Disuniting and dividing by confusing speech and thought.

Now a better day is dawning; God shall make His people
  one,
Shall unite them by His Spirit in the Kingdom of His Son,
Gathering Babel's scattered voices into one united tongue;
So by earth's remotest nations shall one song of praise be
  sung.

Men shall ever hail thy breaking, holy Pentecostal morn:
The Church on thee, as Christ at Christmas, of the Holy
  Ghost was born:
When three thousand vowed obedience to the Son of God
  most High,
Alleluias rose exultant from the armies of the sky.

Glorious band of Twelve Apostles! shall we not their names
  revere?
To their fellowship and doctrine we will steadfastly adhere,

I

On whose sainted heads the Spirit poured His pure
   baptismal fire,
And with wisdom, courage, power, did their tongues and
   hearts inspire.

Praise and glory to the Father, Maker of the earth and
   heaven ;
Praise and glory to the Saviour, Son of God, most high be
   given ;
Praise and glory to the Spirit, Light and Comfort of the soul;
Praise and glory and dominion, while eternal ages roll.

8.   PETER AND JOHN GOING UP TO THE BEAUTIFUL GATE
           OF THE TEMPLE.

St. Peter.   Truly art thou, Sion, a fair place,
               And rightly is this Gate called Beautiful :
            For thence flow streams of mercy and of grace
               Beauty of holiness ! what heart so dull

            As not to feel thy influence divine ?
St. John.   And yet, O Peter, may we not forget
            The words our Master spake about this Shrine :
               The day is coming, when its sun must set

            And all this glorious pile, the towers that crown
               This height, shall of their beauty be bereft,
            These soaring pinnacles, these gates cast down,
               And not one stone upon another left.

St. Peter.   I know it, brother ; but I doubt not still,
               The dew of heaven will light, and blessings wait
            On those who climb with faith this holy hill,
               And enter with glad praise this sacred Gate.

9. Healing of the Lame Man.

The Lame Help, brothers, help ; look on my forlorn plight :
Man.   Lame from my mother's womb, I cannot stand,
          Nor walk ; let me find pity in your sight ;
            In charity extend a helping hand.

St. Peter. Nor gold, nor silver, brother, can I give ;
             But what I can, I give thee ; in the Name
          Of Jesus Christ, by Whom the dead shall live,
             Rise up and walk ; thou art no longer lame.

St. John. Now strengthened are thy feet and ankle-bones :
             Try ; thou canst stand and walk and run and
               leap :
          No longer shalt thou utter feeble moans,
             But praises from thy spirit's deepest deep.

The Lame What strange new power, what wondrous life I
Man.   feel !
             Yes ! I can stand upright, can walk, can run.
St. Peter. Then bless the Lord ; for He alone can heal ;
St. John.   Bless Jesus Christ, the Father's glorious Son.

The Lame Teach me to know the Father and the Son,
Man.   And I will bless them now and evermore.
St. Peter. For ever, then, in His commandments run,
St. John.   And know that God is love ; this Name adore.

All Three. O blest be the Father's glorious Name,
             For ever blest and praised, Whose Name is
               Love ;
          Through endless ages evermore the same,
             Shedding unceasing mercies from above.

10. St. Peter's Address to the People

Ye men of Israel, why this startled gaze ?
Why look ye on us in such wild amaze,
As if by our own word, or human might,
This man were standing whole before your sight ?
Our fathers' God, we publish far and wide,
Jesus, His holy Son, hath glorified :
Whom well ye wot, at the late Paschal Feast,
Pontius, the Governor, would have released :
But ye refused, and asked a murderer,
And made the Prince of Life a sufferer
Of death unmerited : but God hath raised
That Holy One from death, His Name be praised !
We are His witnesses to all mankind,
That they in Him a present God shall find
To save them from all ills : 'tis through His Name
This man ye knew so helpless and so lame
Now stands before you whole, so strong, so blithe—
Erstwhile so crippled, supple now and lithe ;
Faith in His Name hath done this mighty deed :
O let that faith to His obedience lead
Your hearts now penitent, now pricked with grief ;
And He shall send you pardon, peace, relief.
In Him, the ascended Christ, henceforth believe,
Whom, raised aloft, high Heaven must receive,
Till to this earth He shall return once more,
His Father's glorious Kingdom to restore.

IV.

Occasional Poems.

I.

TO THE MEMORY OF A DEAR BROTHER.

[The subject of the following lines, Hugh Jacobs, B A., of Queen's College, Oxford, died, after a rapid decline, at the Vicarage of Cirencester, Gloucestershire, where he had been most kindly received and nursed by the Vicar, the Rev. W. F. Powell. By a coincidence which I could not but deem remarkable, the day of his death was that on which my fellow-passengers and I, on board the " Sir George Seymour "—one of the famous " First Four Ships " which bore the Canterbury Pilgrims from England to New Zealand—first sighted the coast of New Zealand (Dec. 11, 1850), and the day of his funeral was that on which we cast anchor, and landed at Lyttelton (Dec. 17, 1850). I took leave of him on Ryde Pier, in the Isle of Wight, on August 28, 1850, and the first letters I received, after my arrival in New Zealand, brought me the sad and startling news of his death. He was just 23, and, had he lived, would have been ordained at the following Ember-season. These lines were chiefly valued by those who knew him, because they were considered to be " so true."]

DEAR Hugh ! thou darling of thy home and kin,
   My more than brother ! how in every mind,
That did thy gentle, trusting friendship win,
   Is thy unfading memory enshrined !

To know thee was to love, to look upon
　　Was to desire to know ; so sweet a grace
Breathed o'er thy life, such beaming softness shone
　　In those full dark-fringed eyes, that heavenly face.

Yet was thy temper manly : thou wouldst burn
　　At tale of baseness, or at sight of wrong :
Thy generous spirit in contempt would turn
　　From silly affection's mawkish tongue.

Sweet Modesty, chief grace of youth, was thine ;
　　Thy sense and judgment thy short years outran ;
High principle, good taste, did well combine
　　To mark thee for the Christian gentleman.

Ask me whence came these graces?　He alone,
　　Who man's unruly passions doth control,
Can give to those He chooseth for His own
　　Such finely-tempered harmony of soul.

Who love Him, He will love ; who seek Him, find ;
　　Who seek Him early, find most certainly :
Thou soughtest early, and with guileless mind,
　　In earnestness and pure simplicity.

Fervent, but calm, thy piety, scarce known
　　Save by its fruits, by duty's even walk,
By blameless converse, and the holier tone
　　Of opened heart in friendship's deeper talk.

Since of "the pure in heart" 'tis surely told
　　"They shall see God," we cannot doubt that thou
That vision beatific shalt behold
　　In highest heaven, or e'en beholdst it *now*.

Since " blessed are the peace-makers," for such
    Are " called God's children," thou dost surely know
That bliss, since often by love's healing touch
    Thou mad'st sweet peace from sad estrangement grow.

Heart of the parent to the child was turned
    By thy kind intercession, and the child,
Whose breast with strife and discontent had burned,
    Was won to love by thy example mild :

And now thou bind'st us in one sacred sorrow ;
    Though dead, thou speakest, whispering love's increase,
Bidding us from thy early grave to borrow
    Flow'rs of sweet concord, fruits of holy peace.

Hadst thou but lingered to have ta'en thy stand
    Among Christ's ministers, thou wouldst have borne
The torch of truth with no unsteady hand ;
    Thy life had striven thy doctrine to adorn.

But now a better priesthood thou hast gained,
    An everlasting, with the crown and palm,
And pure white robe of righteousness unstained,
    Before the throne of God, and of the Lamb.

" Sure 'tis no loss to die ! " *   O voice of faith !
    Attendant seraphs caught the dying strain—
No loss to such as thou, for Scripture saith,
    To whom " to live is Christ, to die is gain."

To such angelic life fit end was given ;
    Beneath the pastoral roof thy couch was spread ;
Thy life, slow-ebbing, breathed itself to heaven ;
    With scarce a sigh thy gentle spirit fled.

* *Something like these were his last words.*

Thy form as gently from my vision passed,
    When the swift packet bore me from the Pier ;
I gazed, unconscious that I gazed my last ;
    I watched thee turn, slow fade, and disappear.

My course was to this Southern region bound,
    Thine to a better ; when these shores we sighted,
That self-same day thy pilgrimage was crowned
    With glad release, thy toil with rest requited :

And when we anchored in the wished-for port,
    That self-same day they bore thee to thy grave,
Harbour of rest, blest haven of resort
    To heaven-bound pilgrims on the world's rough wave.

As though my course were emblem of thine own,
    Poor earthly type, as when of heaven we dream ;
Faint echo of sweet music, shadow thrown
    Of things above on some low-lying stream.

O ! may I meet thee in those realms above,
    Though all unworthy thy bright lot to share !
O God ! bestow thy grace, for Jesus' love,
    That I, like him, a worthy cross may bear.

October, 1853.

II.

THE MELANESIAN MISSION.

A PARALLEL.

Written at the time when Subscriptions were being raised for building a new "Southern Cross," after the loss of the old one by shipwreck.

WHEN Israel's prophet, heavenward borne,
    His mantle earthward flung,
A younger seer the guerdon claimed,
    And straight to greatness sprung ;

Greatness of those, who trampling self
    Live for the work of God ;
Strong in Whose might, he sought the path
    By his great master trod.

He healed the waters' bitter spring,
    The dead to life restored ;
The heathen chief, his plague-spot cleansed
    The prophet's God adored.

Thankful we own, in these our days,
    A tale in unison ;
The mantle once by Selwyn worn,
    Now fallen on Patteson.*

Through pathless seas behold him seek
    Strange islands unexplored ;
In many differing tongues declare
    Glad tidings of the Lord ;

* Felix opportunitate temporis, *might perhaps be said of this little poem, since the Rev. J. C. Patteson, M.A., had been consecrated Bishop for Melanesia by the Most Rev. G. A. Selwyn, Bishop of New Zealand, and Primate, assisted by Bishops Abraham and Hobhouse, at St. Paul's Church, Auckland, on the Feast of St. Matthias, 1861.*

Heal the soul's bitter springs, to life
　Recall the living dead ;
Sin's plague-spot cleanse, the outcasts bring
　To share the children's bread.

Shall we look idly, coldly on ?
　Extend no helping hand ?
Oh ! pray we, brethren, fervently,
　God speed the Mission-band !

Help we to spread fresh sails, to waft
　Christ's message o'er the main,
That thy mild light, O Southern Cross,
　May glad the Isles again.

Christ's College, July 29th, 1861.

III.

A VISION OF TWO ROADS.

WRITTEN IN TWO SISTERS' ALBUM, BY REQUEST OF THEIR MOTHER.

I saw two roads : a broad and easy one
With gate wide open, wound through flowery meads ;
Fruits rich and tempting hung on either side ;
The air seemed full of dulcet harmonies,
And perfumes wafted on soft summer gales.
What crowds trooped in ! and from their careless throngs
What laughter pealed, and shouts of revelry !
　Fain had I entered, but a warning Voice
Bade me look closer ere I ventured in :
I gazed with keener scrutiny, and then
Amazed I saw, from flowers that seemed so fair,

Poisons distil like dew ; on sunny banks
Serpents lay coiled, and darted sudden wounds
At those who loitered there.   Some gathered fruit ;
They grasped it eagerly ; but, as they ate,
It crumbled into ashes ; still they ate ;
Strong fascination held them powerless.
   Nor was this all ; the air which seemed so sweet
On entering, proved to those who walked there, charged
With noisome vapours, poisoning every breath :
That music, soft at first, became a din
Of raving passions, mingled sounds of hate,
And discontent, and disappointed rage :
Still they went on, some strong enchantment leading.
And now I saw what first I marked not ; all
The path sloped slowly downward ; gleams from Heaven
Flashed on a sign-post, bearing aweful words,
"This leadeth to destruction" ; all might read,
But few attended : some, the danger finding,
Strove early to return ; and many later,
Palled with excess, and sick with deadly wounds,
Rushed back with horror from the dreadful end.
But, ah ! the gate, so wide to enter, grew
Narrower inward, and the passage forth
Most difficult to find, and being found,
More difficult to compass, so that most
Despaired, and to their wallowing turned again.
   " Were this the only road," I said, " how vain,
Dismal and wretched, were the life of man !
Far better surely never to have been ! "
With that I spied a narrow wicket-gate,
Half-hidden, leading to an upward track,
That seemed a steep, impracticable ridge

Betwixt two precipices.   No gay throngs
Passed through this portal ; but one here and there,
Escaping from the crowd, this pathway sought,
Seeing this legend o'er the entrance writ,
"This leadeth Heavenward."   Many sudden slips,
Backslidings, dangerous falls, slow progress, seemed
To mark their painful course ; and some, alas !
Rolled downward to that broad, descending road,
Or took byepaths slow winding to the same.
    But ever and anon a Hand was seen
To raise the fallen, and sustain the weak,
A Hand stretched out from Heaven ; from above
Cool breezes came to fan the toilworn cheek ;
Refreshing dews fell on them from above ;
Light from above oft cheered their lonely way :
All from above, glad welcomes from their home,
And foretastes of their bliss.   When any fell,
I marked how cautious were his after-steps,
And how his very losses turned to gain.
Pleasant and easy seemed the path to those
Who long had walked therein, though difficult
And rugged to the pilgrims of a day.
    Upward it soared, until in fields of light
It lost itself ; and when each traveller reached
That blissful goal of all his toilsome way,
That joy ineffable, that glorious end,
All dangers passed, all sighs for ever hushed,
It seemed as though the heart of Heaven were stirred,
Such shouts of joy rang out ; such seraph songs,
Tuned to the symphony of golden harps,
Pealed jubilant its sapphire courts along.
And now the craving of their souls hath rest,

For they shall see their God, and know as they are known.
" Then welcome toil," I cried, "and welcome pain,
And lonely watch against an inward Foe,
And ceaseless strife with sin, and long suspense,
And all the hardships of a rugged way,
If but at last I win that glorious crown,
Behold my Saviour's face, and share His love,
Amid that radiant throng for evermore."

Christ's College, 1862.

IV

ON A RECENT ATTEMPT TO IMPUGN THE RELATIONS BETWEEN THE DIOCESE OF MELANESIA AND THE CHURCH OF NEW ZEALAND.*

O HOLY shade of Selwyn ! vex thee not :
   The tie that binds us to the Island—See,
   E'en for thine own dear sainted memory,
We will not sever, but will draw the knot
Yet closer, which unites her noble lot
   Of holy enterprise, high destiny,
   With our less rare, yet hallowed, ministry
To flocks long-folded.   Not a single jot
Bate we from Melanesia's granted share
   In our Church-government, nor think to part
   Thy master-pieces twain, linked heart to heart,
The Synod and the Mission.   Who would dare
   To void the seat once filled by Patteson,
   Thy dearer self, and where now sits thy son?

February, 1881.

  * *The reference is to a debate which took place in the General Synod, at the Session held in Christchurch in May,* 1880.

V.

GRACE DESCENDING.

It was an hour of holy communing,
  Heart-kindling aspiration, soul-breathed prayer ;
  A solemn stillness hushed the spell-bound air :
I spake not, saw not, heard not anything ;
Yet I recount no vain imagining,
  But an experience real, what though rare :
  A consciousness came o'er me unaware
Of a sweet presence over-shadowing ;
Down through the night poured a mysterious dew
  Flooding my soul ; an unction from above
  Flushed in an instant all my being through.
O grace ineffable ! O wondrous love !
  Mount up, my soul ! thy loftiest song upraise !
  Melt, grateful heart, dissolve thyself in praise !

March, 1881.

VI.

VALENTINE, BISHOP AND MARTYR.

Could passing sins of earth or follies taint
  The blissful rest of saints in Paradise ;
  Or could we think it vexed the good and wise
That men should use their names without restraint
To shelter vulgar spite, and under feint
  Of chartered trifling vent envenomed lies,
  And wreak a feeble vengeance under guise
Of harmless custom—then, O reverent Saint !
In all the calendar of thee, I trow,

The saddest name must be Saint Valentine :
Not mirthful jesting grieves thee, nor the line
By youthful lover penned, but secret blow
　By malice dealt, and, worst, the treacherous dart
　Dipped in the poison of an envious heart.

St. Valentine's Day, 1882.

———

VII.

THE CASTLE OF DUTY,

OR, THE PALACE OF THE WILL OF GOD.

"St. Catherine of Sienna, in a dialogue she composed on Christian
Perfection, says that amongst many other things her Beloved taught her,
one was, that she ought to shut herself up in the Divine will, as in a most
secure retreat, and live there as a pearl in the shell, or a bee in the hive,
without ever coming forth. That in the beginning, perhaps, she would find
the place very narrow, but afterwards it would be larger, and, without once
coming forth, she might walk there as in the habitations of the blessed, and
obtain in a very short time what, out of that retirement, she would not be
able to compass in a long term of years."

RODRIGUEZ ON CHRISTIAN PERFECTION, Vol. i., p. 340.

I HEWED me out a chamber in a rock :
　Narrow it was, but safe ; quite plain, but pure ;
　Severe its aspect, yet protection sure
It yielded me against the prowling flock
Of noxious beasts ; against rude tempests' shock,
　Dull dripping rain, and sights and sounds that lure :
　Methought at first, "This chamber doth immure
Too prison-like : yet stay ! it will not mock
The firmest trust ; here living, I'll pursue
　My daily task ; here will I ceaseless plod : "
　Then love upsprang ; and lo ! my chamber grew

Into a palace, as by magic rod,
 By day and night : then I the mystery knew—
 The rod was love, that rock the Will of God.

Lent, 1882.

VIII.

A LIFE'S AFTERGLOW.

A Tribute to the Memory of H. J. T.*

Mark well, my friends, that wondrous afterglow :
 Soft violet hues, with mellow golden dyes,
 From day's departing orb, enrich the skies
With lingering sweetness : there is nought, I trow,
In all the realm of nature that can show
 Truer resemblance of the memories
 Abiding with us of the good and wise,
When they have reached the bourn of high and low.
O true of heart !   O friend of many a year !
 Thy gracious influence shall linger long
 About the places that have known thee here—
Thy purpose high, deep reverence, judgment strong ;
 Thy playful wit, to tender memory dear ;
 Thy love of justice, and thy hate of wrong.

Oamaru, May, 1884.

The Hon. Henry John Tancred, first Chancellor of the University of New Zealand.

IX.

A PASSENGER'S NIGHT THOUGHTS ON BOARD THE R.M.S. TONGARIRO.

(Off the Horn, May 29th, 1890, somewhere about 3 a.m., and on subsequent nights.)

THY form may seem unwieldy, and thy voice
A hideous compound of repulsive sounds,
Thy very name uncouth and barbarous,
Thou heaving, panting monster of the deep.
A hundred demons dancing overhead
Could hardly match that horrid ceaseless din,
The gurgling rush, the well-nigh maddening rattle
Of thy propeller battling with the waves.
Yet have I learnt to love thee, for thou art
Our bearer onward to the dear old land
Which none can e'er forget, or cease to love,
Who drew their earliest breath 'neath England's sky.
For this I do esteem thy bitter, sweet,
Thy throbs, the pulses of ecstatic hope,
Thy maddening noises, transports of delight,
Thy hideous discords, sweetest harmony.
Fain would I count thy throbbings one by one,
As each one speeds us onward to our home,
As schoolboys count the days till tasks shall cease :
And, as benighted travellers rejoice,
When they have wandered from the homeward track,
To hear far sounds which guide them to their bourn,
E'en though those noises speak not love but strife,
So will I welcome thy most hideous din,
For that it prophesies of joys to come,

K

When waiting friends shall greet us eye to eye.
   Then bear us, friendly monster, giant kind,
Regardless of our brief discomfort, on,
And bring us to the country of our sires.
   And now, O gracious heavenly Father, make
This ship to me a parable of life :
Teach me to suffer sweetly, patiently,
The hardships of this fretful pilgrimage,
The long unrest of life, its discords, woes,
Its never-ceasing tumult, chance and change,
So Thou wilt bring me, at my journey's end,
To that blest haven, where we all would be.

X.

A JUBILEE HYMN.

DEDICATED TO HER MOST GRACIOUS MAJESTY, QUEEN VICTORIA.

FOR fifty years of ampler peace
   Than ever blessed an earthly reign—
Peace, coupled with the realm's increase—
   Fair peace, without dishonour's stain ;
Their grateful hymn Thy people raise ;
Thy holy Name we bless and praise.

For fifty years of temporal good ;
   For equal laws, for health diffused ;
For Nature better understood ;
   Her forces in man's service used ;
Their grateful hymn Thy people raise ;
Thy holy Name we bless and praise.

For fifty years of widening trade,
   And flag in every port unfurled ;
Fair colonies—foundations laid
   Of daughter-states in all the world ;
Their grateful hymn Thy people raise ;
Thy holy Name we bless and praise.

For fifty years of blameless life—
   A throned example—beaming bright
Yet gently—pattern mother, wife—
   To every home a beacon-light ;
Their grateful hymn Thy people raise ;
Thy holy Name we bless and praise.

For fifty years of quickened zeal ;
   For deeds of glowing piety ;
For broadening love of hearts that feel
   A longing hope of unity ;
Their grateful hymn Thy people raise ;
Thy holy Name we bless and praise.

Long live our gracious Queen ! and may
   The gifts that in past years were given,
Be earnest of a glorious Day,
   That we with her may share in heaven !
So we with her through endless days
Thy holy Name will bless and praise.   Amen.

Christchurch, June 20th, 1887.

The dedication of the above Hymn was graciously accepted by Her Majesty. It was sung with great enthusiasm in Christchurch Cathedral on the Fiftieth Anniversary of the Queen's Accession, and again on Sunday, June 26th, to a very spirited tune composed by G. F. Tendall, *Esq., Mus. Bac., Oxon, Organist and Choirmaster of the Cathedral.*

www.ingramcontent.com/pod-product-compliance
Lightning Source LLC
Chambersburg PA
CBHW021114020726
47500CB00003B/749